THE FALSE GOSPEL OF BAPTISMAL REGENERATION IN THE LUTHERAN CHURCH AND CHRIST'S CALL TO SAVING FAITH

Curtis Braun

New Harbor Press

New Harbor Press

1601 Mt Rushmore Rd, Ste 3288

Rapid City, SD 57701

www.newharborpress.com

Ordering Information:

Quantity sales. Special discounts are available on quantity purchases by corporations, associations, and others. For details, contact the "Special Sales Department" at the address above.

The False Gospel/Braun —1st ed.

ISBN 978-1-63357-415-1

First edition: 10 9 8 7 6 5 4 3 2 1

Contents

Preface

As you read through this book, you'll notice that the chapters will not only address the specific verses which are used to support baptismal regeneration but will also exposit previous verses and chapters to help understand the verse. This book will pay attention to the language, culture, geography, and history to help exposit the meaning of the verse. Likewise, I've tried to support the Scriptures using the Synthesis Principle knowing that the Bible does not contradict itself. If there is a passage of Scripture that contradicts a truth taught elsewhere in the Scriptures, then it would be an incorrect interpretation. The Scripture that I've used in this book is compared with other Scripture to help uncover the full meaning of texts and understand the false gospel of baptismal regeneration.

Since this book is specifically addressing the false gospel of baptismal regeneration in The Lutheran Church—Missouri Synod (LCMS), there is a chapter addressing the error in this Synod's teaching. However, the LCMS is not the only church that teaches baptismal regeneration. There are several other Lutheran churches that teach baptismal regeneration. Additionally, the Catholic Church also teaches baptismal regeneration as well as many other churches. This book is to serve the purpose of explaining why baptismal regeneration is a false teaching and a false gospel. This book will also address key doctrines that relate to soteriology such as regeneration, repentance, and saving faith. Lastly, the book will end with a stern warning to those who should preach the false gospel of baptismal regeneration.

The issue that this book will present is that Martin Luther did not properly separate water baptism and baptism with the Holy Spirit. This error led to a misunderstanding of the baptism with the Holy Spirit which led to a misunderstanding of regeneration/being born again which has led to an errant understanding of water baptism in salvation. This book will highlight this fatal misunderstanding. Martin Luther erroneously replaced regeneration with baptismal regeneration by not properly separating water baptism with baptism with the Holy Spirit.

With all this being said, why would I endeavor to write this book? I was everything the Bible said about those who would not inherit the kingdom of God. I was the blaspheming, fornicating, adulterer, porn-addicted, lying, manipulating, selfish, thief. The verses below capture my nature, my will, and my walk of life before Christ saved me:

- 1 Corinthians 6:9–10—Or do you not know that wrongdoers will not inherit the kingdom of God? Do not be deceived: Neither the sexually immoral nor idolaters nor adulterers nor men who have sex with men nor thieves nor the greedy nor drunkards nor slanderers nor swindlers will inherit the kingdom of God?
- Ephesians 5:3–6—But among you there must not be a hint of sexual immorality, or of any kind of impurity, or of greed, because these are improper for God's holy people. Nor should there be obscenity, foolish talk or coarse joking, which are out of place, but rather thanksgiving. For of this you can be sure: No immoral, impure, or greedy person—such a person is an idolater—has any inheritance in the kingdom of Christ and of God. Let no one deceive you with empty words, for because of such things God's wrath comes on those who are disobedient
- Romans 6:20—When you were slaves to sin, you were free from the control of righteousness.

After my conversion I reached out to family members and shared the good news that Christ saved me. In fact, I would make it a point to tell people of my former way of life and what Christ had done to me. I had no regard for my reputation. What mattered is that people knew that Christ could save the greatest sinners.

However, some of the saddest and most disappointing moments would come when dealing with LCMS pastors or members. I would share how God had saved me and I would hear the following:

- Me: Jesus saved me. I realize that I was never a Christian.
  Anonymous LCMS: You've always been saved and believed. You had the promise of baptism and the Holy Spirit was in there somewhere working.
- Me: I was recently saved. I was an adulterer, addicted to pornography, and the Lord saved me.
  Anonymous LCMS: You know when I was saved? July 16, 1954. The day I was baptized.
- Me: We need to warn people of the narrow gate and few be it that find it and many being on the broad road that leads to destruction (Matthew 7:13–14).
  Anonymous LCMS: We're not going to preach or teach that.
- Me: We need to warn people that they could be baptized and confirmed members of a church and be self-deceived into thinking they have saving faith (Matthew 7:21–23).
  Anonymous LCMS: We're not going to preach or teach that.
- Me: The Bible is full of warnings where people think they are saved, but are really self-deceived (Matthew 7:13–14—Two Gates and Two Roads, Matthew 7:21-23—True and False Disciples, Matthew 7:24–27—Two Foundations).
  Anonymous LCMS: You're mixing law and grace.

- Me: Aren't you concerned that this person has been living in fornication for several years with no signs of repentance?
  Anonymous LCMS: They are justified by faith not by works
- Me: Aren't you concerned that this person has been addicted to drugs for several years and is now possibly committing adultery?
  Anonymous LCMS: You can't mix law and grace together.
- Me: This person didn't seem to show any fruits that Scripture talks about (Luke 3, John 15).
  Anonymous LCMS: Just remember, they were a baptized child of God.

I was dead in adultery. I was dead in pornography. In fact, I had reached out to a company that assisted in suicides to help me end my life. My marriage was falling apart and I saw no hope for my life. I was dead, lost, and damned. However, God saved me by His grace in my thirties. God caused me to be born again. God gave me the gift of repentance. God gave me the gift of faith. God has been so merciful and compassionate to me. God has illumined me to the truth of His Word. Therefore, I've written this book. I was raised in the LCMS and, through studying Scripture after my conversion, came to understand the false teaching and false gospel of baptismal regeneration. I came to understand what a fatal teaching this is in the church. This book is for the glory of God and to spread His truth. He must increase and I must decrease (John 3:30)!

Acknowledgments

Jesus Christ—To my Lord, Savior, and God who purchased me with His blood and saved me. To the only wise God to whom will be all glory and honor forever and ever.

Laura—For being my wife and staying with me through my infidelity and being patient and loving to me. I have much to learn from you on love and patience. Stand firm in the faith and be steadfast, immovable, always abounding in the work of the Lord.

Pax—Contend earnestly for the once for all delivered to the saints, faith. Jesus is everything. Choose Jesus and grow in your fear and admonition of the Lord. Love the Lord your God with all your heart, and with all your soul, and with all your mind, and with all your strength. Fight the good fight of faith.

Keryx—Contend earnestly for the once for all delivered to the saints, faith. Jesus is everything. Choose Jesus and grow in your fear and admonition of the Lord. Love the Lord your God with all your heart, and with all your soul, and with all your mind, and with all your strength. Fight the good fight of faith.

Pastor Randy—Thank you for not breaking the bruised reed or snuffing out the smoldering wick. Thank you for being onc approved by God who has no need to be ashamed, rightly handling the word of truth.

To my parents—Thank you for sacrificing to put me through Lutheran education and raising me. Your sacrifice is an example of sacrificing for Christian education.

CHAPTER 1

Jesus on the Doctrine of Regeneration

John 3:3—Jesus responded and said to him, "Truly, truly, I say to you, unless someone is born again he cannot see the kingdom of God."

The doctrine of regeneration is a doctrine that is significantly missing in modern Christianity. In fact, there are many protestant groups that can altogether leave this doctrine out or inaccurately describe it. Ensuring that this doctrine is explained clearly, accurately, and articulately as possible within the confines of Scripture aids in understanding salvation, but also refuting baptismal regeneration. Having a good definition of regeneration/born again/born from above will clarify this doctrine. The definition of *regeneration* would be as follows: **Regeneration is the sovereign monergistic work of God the Holy Spirit in giving spiritual life to spiritually dead and sinful man so that man is enabled to repent and respond in saving faith to Jesus Christ.** The doctrine of regeneration can most succinctly be found in the book of John where Nicodemus visits Jesus. A correct understanding and verse by verse exposition of John 3:1–10 will help our understanding of how true biblical regeneration has been replaced with the false teaching and false gospel of baptismal regeneration.

John 3:1—Now there was a man of the Pharisees, named Nicodemus, a ruler of the Jews.

Two of the questions that must be answered are: What are the Pharisees and what does it mean that Nicodemus was a ruler of the Jews? *Pharisees* were the religious teachers during the time of Christ. At the time of Christ, Josephus records that there were about six thousand Pharisees in Israel. The term *Pharisee* comes from the term "separated." Pharisees are depicted in a very negative light in the New Testament, but during this specific time in Israel, they were seen as the conservative religious leaders. They were zealous to keep the law and they were the experts on Scripture. If we look at Paul's description of what a Pharisee looked like, we get a small glimpse into the thoughts and life of a Pharisee. Paul describes being circumcised on the eighth day which could be understood as receiving the covenant sign of faith (Romans 4:9–12, Philippians 3:5). Paul describes being of the tribe of Benjamin which was the tribe that produced the first king of Israel, King Saul, and was an esteemed tribe (Philippians 3:5). Paul describes his knowledge of the law as being second to none among the Pharisees (Philippians 3:5). Paul describes his zeal for Judaism as persecuting the church or rather persecuting any other religion that sets itself up against Judaism (Philippians 3:6). Lastly, Paul describes his external righteousness based on the law as faultless (Philippians 3:6).

Pharisees were meticulous about preserving both the Old Testament Scripture as well as oral tradition. Nicodemus was not only a Pharisee, but he was also a member of the Jewish Sanhedrin. There were two classes of Jewish courts which were called *Sanhedrin*. There was the Great Sanhedrin and the Lesser Sanhedrin. A Lesser Sanhedrin of twenty-three judges was appointed to sit as a tribunal in each city, but there was only supposed to be one Great Sanhedrin of seventy-one judges which, among other roles, acted as the Supreme Court. The Great Sanhedrin would take appeals from cases which were passed to them by lesser courts. To put it in modern terms, there were state Supreme Courts and Federal Supreme Courts, and Nicodemus was a member of the Federal Supreme Court. There were seventy one judges on the Great Sanhedrin in the case of an even vote so that the seventy-first member could be the tiebreaker. In the modern US era, judges that are on the Supreme Court not only have attended the best law schools, but they have also served on smaller circuits, gained experience, and are considered experts in the law. In the same way, Pharisees were experts in Old Testament Scripture and the law. They were knowledgeable in Scripture and were considered the premier teachers in Israel. In summation, Nicodemus is an expert in Scripture and the law and has attained one of the highest positions in Jewish culture and religion.

John 3:2—This man came to Jesus at night and said to him, "Rabbi, we know that You have come from God as a teacher; for no one can do these signs that You do unless God is with him."

Nicodemus, a member of the Sanhedrin, comes to Jesus in the cover of night. There may be many speculations made on why Nicodemus came by himself at night. Most likely it was because he was concerned over his salvation (see commentary on verse 3), but it is important to notice the Savior's open arms. Christ is a gracious and merciful Lord. Though He would go on and oppose the Pharisees numerous times, Christ still makes time for a teacher coming at night. Nicodemus approaches Jesus in a respectful manner and calls Him "Rabbi." The lexicon describes *Rabbi* as literally meaning "great in number," probably referring to great scriptural knowledge. It also literally meant "My great one; my honorable sir." Nicodemus acknowledges that the Pharisees know that Jesus is a teacher that has come from God. Although Jesus was early on in His ministry, by this time Jesus had turned water into wine and had cleared the temple courts at the time of the Jewish Passover. The miracle of turning water into wine had never been performed. Therefore, Nicodemus knew that Jesus must have been sent by God given these signs.

John 3:3—Jesus responded and said to him, "Truly, truly, I say to you, unless someone is born again he cannot see the kingdom of God."

It seems odd that Jesus doesn't answer or respond to Nicodemus' greeting, but rather launches into a teaching and explanation of being born again. It's very likely that Jesus knew Nicodemus' heart and his thoughts since Jesus knew all people and knew what was in mankind (John 2:24–25). Therefore, it is reasonable to surmise that Nicodemus had come to Jesus because he had questions on salvation and perhaps even his own salvation. Jesus begins His teaching on regeneration by saying "Truly, truly" or rather, "Amen, amen." The lexicon describes "amen" by stating that *amen* means that "what is about to be said is sure and certain." It is also used at the beginning of a statement to introduce something of pivotal importance. As R. C. Sproul has said, "Whenever we read in the text of Scripture our Lord giving a statement that is prefaced by the double 'amen,' it is time to pay close attention and be ready to give our response with a double amen to it."

The first thing that Jesus says is, "Truly, truly, I say to you, unless someone is born again he cannot see the kingdom of God." What a loaded statement of truth! Understanding this statement is critical so it's important to analyze it piece by piece.

What does Jesus mean by being *born again*? In the original language, *born again* is *"gennethe anothen." Gennethe* is derived from *gennao* which means "to beget, or to bring forth." It is used to describe being born. The Greek word *anothen* can also be translated as "from above." When putting both words together, *born again* can also be translated "born from above." There are a few cross-references to consider with the word *anothen*. In John 3:31, Jesus says, "The one who comes from above is above all;

the one who is from the earth belongs to the earth, and speaks as one from the earth." When Jesus says, "The one who comes from above," He is referring to Himself coming from heaven or from above. In John 19:11, Jesus says, "You would have no power over me if it were not given to you from above." Once again, the word *anothen* is referring to something coming from God or heaven. In James 1:17, the author says, "Every good and perfect gift is from above, coming from the Father of the heavenly light, who does not change like shifting shadows." This is another example of the word *anothen* referring to something coming from God or heaven.

The next phrase to dissect is *cannot see*. In the original language it says, "*ou dynatai idein*." The word *ou* is translated as "not." *Dynatai* is derived from the root word *dunamai* which means "to be able" or "to have power." The last word, *idein*, is derived from the root word *horao* which means to "see," "perceive," "discern," or, metaphorically, "to spiritually see with inward spiritual perception." The translation into English "cannot see" is a very good translation. Another way to accurately translate this whole phrase "*ou dynatai idein*" would be to say, "has no power or ability to see or perceive."

The next question is: What is the kingdom of God? Some theologians have described this as the "sphere of salvation," "God's reign through God's people over God's place," "salvation," and more. Any of these descriptions would be appropriate. There is a kingdom, which means there is a King. Since it's the kingdom of God, God is the King over those who enter His kingdom. These individuals who enter the kingdom of God are those who have inherited eternal life and salvation. Hence, we understand the *kingdom of God* as those who inherit salvation and enter His kingdom. In the book of Matthew, it is called the "kingdom of heaven." The *kingdom of heaven* expression carries the same meaning as the *kingdom of God* as it describes the spiritual realm over which the Lord reigns as King.

So, let's put all these phrases together in verse 3. Jesus says, "Truly, truly, I say to you, unless someone is born again he cannot see the kingdom of God." I will take some liberty to say the same thing but in a different way that carries the same meaning:

- Most assuredly and most certainly, unless you are born from above, you have no power to see the sphere of salvation.
- This is the truth, unless you are born from above, you cannot spiritually understand how to enter the spiritual realm over which the Lord reigns.
- Pay attention to this important truth, unless you are born from above, you have no ability to see and understand how to be saved.
- Most assuredly and most certainly, unless you are born from above, you have no ability to see how to enter the kingdom of heaven through saving faith in Christ.

Notice here that being born from above is a necessity to enter the kingdom of God. Without the spiritual regeneration, no man can see the call of repentance and faith (Mark 1:15). Also note that unless you are born from above or have a spiritual rebirth, you can't see the kingdom of heaven and, thus, won't be able to enter the kingdom of heaven. Also note that this is a personal spiritual rebirth. Ask yourself: What ability do you have to be born from above? Ask yourself: What role did you have in your physical birth? Ask yourself: What role did you have in your conception? If you had no role in your physical birth or conception, what role do you have in your spiritual birth? The undeniable answer is that just as you had no role in your physical birth, you have no role in your spiritual birth.

Also pay attention to what Jesus just told Nicodemus. Nicodemus was at the highest religious level in Judaism and Jesus tells him that he must be born again before he can even perceive or see the kingdom of God. In other words, he's saying, "Nicodemus, all your religious achievement, all your education, all your knowledge, all your righteous works, all your ceremonies, all your Sabbaths, all your sacrifices, all your law keeping, all your prayers, all your Passovers, all your rituals, and all your efforts to enter into the kingdom amount to nothing. You need to start all over again because what you have falls short. God is not impressed by your religious achievements. All your years of apostate Judaism is worth nothing. If you want to enter the kingdom of God, you need to start all over and be born from above." This is what Jesus is telling Nicodemus.

Also take care to note that if you have not been born from above, you are spiritually dead. If you have not been born from above, you will not have spiritual life when you die.

John 3:4—Nicodemus said to Him, "How can a person be born when he is old? He cannot enter his mother's womb a second time and be born, can he?"

Nicodemus understands what Jesus just said. Nicodemus understands that Jesus is using a physical example to explain a spiritual reality. Nicodemus understands that it is impossible to be physically born a second time. There is no example of anyone ever being physically born again so Nicodemus knows that physical rebirth is impossible. Therefore, Jesus' example is showing Nicodemus that if physical rebirth is impossible, how much more impossible is it to be born from above? How can a man physically make a physical rebirth happen? Likewise, what can a man do to be born from above? What prayer can he pray? What sacrament can he partake in? What law can he keep? What good work can he do? He could also ask more questions about physical rebirth: What role did he play in his first birth? Did he have any say when he was conceived? Did he have any say what day he was born? Did he have any say in his gender? Did he have any say on how long he stayed in the womb?

When looking into Scripture, surely Nicodemus would know Psalm 139:13–15, "For you created my innermost parts; you wove me in my mother's womb. I will give thanks to You, because I am awesomely and wonderfully made; wonderful are your works, and my soul knows it very well. My frame was not hidden from You when I was made in secret, and skillfully formed in the depths of the earth. Your eyes have seen my formless substance; and in Your book were written all the days that were ordained for me, when as yet there was not one of them." So, just as Nicodemus had no part in his physical birth, he would surely have no part in a spiritual birth. Jesus is showing that being born from above is simply a monergistic work that man has no control over and Nicodemus understands the impossibility of rebirth by Jesus' question.

John 3:5—Jesus answered, "Truly, truly, I say to you, unless someone is born of water and the Spirit, he cannot enter the kingdom of God."

Jesus is about to make another statement that is of critical importance. As we learned earlier, it's time to pay attention because what He is about to say is an essential truth as triggered by the double amen. Jesus says, "Unless someone is born of water and the Spirit, he cannot enter the kingdom of God." Since we have taken time to understand what the kingdom of God is, we need to understand what it means to be born of water and the Spirit. Commentaries from different theologians and denominations look to this passage as clear evidence that this is a reference to Christian baptism. They see water and they see Spirit and conclude that the Holy Spirit and the Word is in the water which yields the net effect of the word being connected to the water which, thus, creates saving faith.

Not only is this a wrong interpretation of Scripture, but this is also a false Gospel which will be addressed later. Jesus has just gotten done explaining that you must be born from above to see the kingdom of God and Nicodemus understands that this second birth is out of his control. Jesus is about to double down on the emphasis of the new birth being a monergistic act of God. Additionally, Nicodemus would not have thought of baptism as Jesus had not yet instituted Christian baptism. Nicodemus would not have thought of John the Baptist's baptism either as John's baptism was for a radical repentance which the Pharisees rejected (Luke 7:30). John himself said in Luke 3:16, "John answered them all, 'I baptize you with water. But one who is more powerful than I will come, the straps of whose sandals I am not worthy to untie. He will baptize you with the Holy Spirit and fire.'"

Jesus not only affirmed John's message of repentance, but also affirmed John's other messages when He says in Matthew 11:11, "Truly I tell you, among those born of women there has not risen anyone greater than John the Baptist." What a stunning statement by John which Jesus affirms. He is stating that he can only baptize with water but has no power to baptize with the Holy Spirit. Furthermore, Nicodemus would not have been thinking that he just needed to undergo one more ceremony, ritual, or perform one more good work as Jesus is emphasizing being born from above. Nicodemus and the Pharisees believed that you became ceremonially unclean by not washing one's hands prior to eating (Matthew 15:1-9). Nicodemus would have been very familiar with all of the Old Testament water purification rituals. Nicodemus would have been very familiar with the Mikvah water purification rituals and ceremonial cleansings. Nicodemus would have been very familiar with the Mikvah purification rituals as it relates to converting to Judaism. Let us take note that no one except Jesus can baptize with the Holy Spirit. In fact, in verse 8, Jesus will confirm this fact that man cannot control the Holy Spirit. Therefore, this cannot be in reference to Christian baptism.

So, what is Jesus trying to say? Remember that Nicodemus was advanced in Judaism and, as Jesus said in verse 10, "You are the teacher of Israel." Nicodemus, you are *the* teacher which is a definite article. Jesus says, you aren't *"a"* teacher which is an indefinite article, but definite article *"the"* teacher. Jesus is telling Nicodemus to follow along. Jesus is saying, "You should know what I'm saying when I say, 'born of water and the spirit.'" Jesus is pointing Nicodemus to the New Covenant promise of Ezekiel 36. Although the Scripture of Ezekiel 36 is being spoken to Israel, it is true for every believer. Ezekiel 36:24–27 says, "For I will take you from the nations, and gather you from all the lands; and I will bring you into your own land. Then I will sprinkle clean **water** on you, and you will be clean; I will cleanse you from all your filthiness and from all your idols. Moreover, I will give you a new heart and put a new spirit within you; and I will remove the heart of stone from your flesh and give you a heart of flesh. And I will put my **Spirit** within you and bring it about that you walk in My statutes, and are careful and follow My ordinances." This is most certainly where Jesus is pointing Nicodemus.

Nicodemus would have and should have been aware of this passage of Scripture as it pointed to Israel's restoration, and he should have been aware of the personal pronouns in this portion of Scripture. In these three short verses, the LORD uses the personal pronoun *"I"* seven times. He is indicating that this salvation will strictly be a work of God. This work of salvation will be a one-sided affair. The LORD God is going to perform a mighty act of salvation for His name's sake. To understand Jesus' statement of being born of water and the Spirit, it's important to understand Ezekiel 36:24–27.

In Ezekiel 36:24, the LORD says, "For **I** will take you from the nations, and gather you from all the lands; and **I** will bring you into your own land." In this portion the LORD is pointing to separation or holiness. This is to say that when God justifies, God also sanctifies. It's to say when God gives the man the gift of faith and repentance and brings him through the narrow gate, God immediately places that man on the narrow road (Matthew 7:13–14). It is to say that when God justifies a man, He will keep that man sanctified until He ultimately glorifies that man (Romans 8:29–30). Let us firmly remember Ezekiel 36:23 where the LORD says, "And I will vindicate the holiness of My great name which has been profaned among the nations, which you have profaned among them. Then the nations will know that I am the LORD," declares the LORD God, "when I show Myself holy among you in their sight." When God regenerates and saves a man, He is proven holy among men and the nations. That is to say that the salvific work of God is so holy and amazing, that although unregenerate man may not fully understand the salvation that took place, they will marvel and awe at the transforming and regenerative work of God who puts the life of God in the soul of a man. It is to say that God always acts first! It is to say that God always acts first! You can almost hear Jesus saying, "Nicodemus aren't you familiar with Ezekiel 16:1–8?":

"The word of the Lord came to me: "Son of man, confront Jerusalem with her detestable practices and say, 'This is what the Sovereign Lord says to Jerusalem: Your ancestry and birth were in the land of the Canaanites; your father was an Amorite and your mother a Hittite. On the day you were born your cord was not cut, nor were you washed with water to make you clean, nor were you rubbed with salt or wrapped in cloths. No one looked on you with pity or had compassion enough to do any of these things for you. Rather, you were thrown out into the open field, for on the day you were born you were despised. 'Then I passed by and saw you kicking about in your blood, and as you lay there in your blood I said to you, "Live!" I made you grow like a plant of the field. You grew and developed and entered puberty. Your breasts had formed and your hair had grown, yet you were stark naked. "'Later I passed by, and when I looked at you and saw that you were old enough for love, I spread the corner of my garment over you and covered your naked body. I gave you my solemn oath and entered into a covenant with you, declares the Sovereign Lord, and you became mine."

It's as if Jesus is telling Nicodemus, "It's always been about God acting on His own initiative and will." It's as if Jesus is saying, "You've never done anything to earn my favor. Nicodemus, don't you see that you were not a nation, until I made you a nation? Nicodemus, don't you remember when I spoke to Elijah and told him that I have reserved seven thousand in Israel—all whose knees have not bowed down to Baal and whose mouths have not kissed him (1 Kings 19:18)? Nicodemus, don't you know that I'm the one who set apart Israel for myself? Nicodemus, don't you see that I alone separate men unto myself?"

Ezekiel 36:25—The LORD says, "Then I will sprinkle clean water on you, and you will be clean; I will cleanse you from all your filthiness and from all your idols."

Once again, notice the personal pronoun of "*I.*" **I** will sprinkle clean water on you and **I** will cleanse you. The question to ask is: What is this reference to water? After David had been confronted for his sin of adultery and murder by the prophet Nathan, he penned Psalm 51, which gives us insight into this water and cleansing reference. In Psalm 51:1–2, he says, "Be gracious to me, God, according to Your faithfulness; According to the greatness of Your compassion, wipe out my wrongdoings. Wash me thoroughly from my guilt and cleanse me from my sin." In verse 7, he says, "Purify me with hyssop, and I will be clean; cleanse me, and I will be whiter than snow." No theologian would *exposit*, or try to reason, that David is asking the LORD for a bath, a shower, or a ceremonial washing. No, the washing that David is asking for is the washing away and cleansing of sins. He is asking for personal forgiveness from the LORD. He is asking that the LORD would not look at his sins but turn away from them. He is asking the LORD for mercy and compassion and not to deal with him according to justice. He is also asking to be cleansed. In the Hebrew, this word is *taher*, which means "to be clean or pure." In context, David is saying, "Cleanse me and purge me from my immorality. Only you can make me morally clean. Only you can cleanse my murderous and adulterous heart. I don't need a physical bath, LORD! I need you to cleanse the filth in my heart."

In verse 10 of Psalm 51, David cries out for the same thing, "Create in me a clean heart, God, and renew a steadfast spirit within me." Once again paraphrasing David, "LORD I have no ability to change my heart. I have no ability to keep your laws. LORD without you cleansing my heart and renewing my spirit, I am hopeless." In verse 25 of Ezekiel, the LORD is saying this very thing. The LORD is saying that He is the one who will act to forgive sins. He is the one who will purify us from our sins. He is the one that that will cleanse us from our filthiness and idols. Note here that this is not just a reference to forgiveness of sins. This is also a promise to purify us morally from our sins and idols. Again, what the LORD is saying is that this cleansing and purification is not just forgiveness of sins, but it's a continual work of God to rid one's life of sin. Nicodemus should have known this. You can almost hear Jesus saying to Nicodemus, "Nicodemus, don't you know that it is God who forgives sins? Nicodemus, don't you know that it is God who cleanses people from their sins? Don't you know that unless God cleanses someone from the inside, he cannot be clean before God? Nicodemus, don't you know that external water cannot take away the stain of sin, but only God can remove the stain of sin? Nicodemus, won't you learn from David and see that the cleansing you really need is from the heart? Nicodemus, God is the one who sprinkles the clean water and who cleanses you."

Ezekiel 36:26—The LORD says, "I will give you a new heart and put a new spirit in you; I will remove from you your heart of stone and give you a heart of flesh."

Let's remember that Jesus just said to Nicodemus that you must be born of water and the Spirit. Verse 25 captures the water and verse 27 captures the Spirit but sandwiched in between the water and the Spirit is verse 26 that talks about the LORD giving a new heart and a new spirit. So, what does this mean? When the

LORD says He will give a new heart and a new spirit, He is saying that He isn't going to help man be a better person, or more moral, or to help him love Him just a little more. No, He is saying that He is going to change man's very nature and who man is. Often times, the heart and the spirit encapsulate man's intellect, emotions/affections, and will (i.e., his whole being). What the LORD is saying is that He's going to change man's intellect so man will know the LORD. He will change man's emotions and affections so that man's affections will be towards the LORD and what the LORD loves. What the LORD hates, man will hate and what the LORD loves, man will love. The LORD will also change man's will so that man's disposition will be inclined to do the will of the LORD.

What is a heart of stone? A *heart of stone* is an inanimate object. A heart that has no life. You can kick a stone, you can shock a stone, you can scream at a stone, but the stone will not respond. The heart of stone does not respond to divine stimuli or God's Word. A *heart of flesh* is a heart that is alive. The heart of flesh is responsive. The heart of flesh has a pulse. The heart of flesh responds to divine stimuli or God's Word. What then is the spirit? The *spirit* is the innermost part of man. In Genesis 6:5, it says, "The LORD saw how great the wickedness of the human race had become on the earth, and that every inclination of the thoughts of the human heart was only evil all the time." That is the inclination of man. That is man's heart and spirit. Man's heart and spirit is only evil and inclined towards evil all the time. In Jeremiah 13:23, the LORD says, "Can an Ethiopian change his skin or a leopard its spots? Neither can you do good who are accustomed to doing evil." Once again, the LORD is saying man cannot change his evil disposition no more than a leopard can change his skin or an Ethiopian change his skin. It's not possible. The LORD says of man's heart in Jeremiah 17:9, "The heart is deceitful above all things and beyond cure. Who can understand it?" Once again, verse 26 is sandwiched between water and the spirit and Jesus is drawing Nicodemus to this sovereign act of God which changes a man's very being and imparts spiritual life.

Ontology is the study of being or the nature of being. A man will follow his nature. A pig will always lay in its filth. A bird will fly south when winter comes. A man will always choose evil because that is his nature. The changing of one's being is only accomplished by the sovereign work of God. Man can't change his nature. In Ezekiel 11:19–20, the LORD makes a similar promise and says, "I will give them an undivided heart and put a new spirit in them; I will remove from them their heart of stone and give them a heart of flesh. Then they will follow my decrees and be careful to keep my laws. They will be my people and I will be their God." In Jeremiah 31:31–34, the LORD makes a new covenant promise in saying:

"'The days are coming,' declares the LORD, 'when I will make a new covenant with the people of Israel and with the people of Judah. It will not be like the covenant I made with their ancestors when I took them by the hand to lead them out of Egypt, because they broke my covenant, though I was a husband to them," declares the LORD. "This is the covenant I will make with the people of Israel after that time," declares the LORD. "I will put my law in their minds and write it on their hearts. I will be their God, and they will be my people. No longer will they teach their neighbor, or say to one another, 'Know the LORD,' because they will all know me, from the least of them to the greatest," declares the LORD. "For I will forgive their wickedness and will remember their sins no more." In Jeremiah 24:7 the LORD gives another promise of changing man where He says, "I will also give them a heart to know Me, for I am the LORD; and they will be My people, and I will be their God, for they will return to Me wholeheartedly." In Jeremiah 32:38-40 the LORD continues with His promise to change and regenerate man where He says, "They shall be My people, and I will be their God; and I will give them one heart and one way, so that they will fear Me always, for their own good and for the good of their children after them. I will make an everlasting covenant with them that I will not turn away from them, to do them good; and I will put the fear of Me in their hearts, so that they will not turn away from me." The amazing work of the LORD to completely change man's intellect, emotions, and will are stunning when you combine Ezekiel 11:19-20, Jeremiah 24:7, Jeremiah 32:38-40, Ezekiel 36:24-27, Jeremiah 31:33-34. Let's put all of these verses together in one statement to get an understanding of the regenerating and saving work the LORD does where He completely changes man's intellect, emotions/affections, will, and nature so man is thus inclined to repent and trust in Jesus Christ:

And I will give them one heart, and put a new spirit within them. And I will remove the heart of stone from their flesh and give them a heart of flesh, so that they will walk in My statutes, and keep My ordinances and do them. Then they will be My people, and I shall be their God. I will also give them a heart to know Me, for I am the LORD; and they will be My people, and I will be their God, for they will return to Me wholeheartedly. They shall be My people, and I will be their God; and I will give them one heart and one way, so that they will fear Me always, for their own good and for the good of their children after them. I will make an everlasting covenant with them that I will not turn away from them, to do them good; and I will put the fear of Me in their hearts, so that they will not turn away from Me. For I will take you from the nations, and gather you from all the lands; and I will bring you into your own land. Then I will sprinkle clean water on you, and you will be clean; I will cleanse you from all your filthiness and from all your idols. Moreover, I will give you a new heart and put a new spirit within you; and I will remove the heart of stone from your flesh and give you a heart of flesh. And I will put my Spirit within you and bring it about that you walk in My statutes, and are careful and follow my ordinances. For this is the covenant which I will make with the house of Israel after those days, "declares the LORD: "I will put My law within them and write it on their heart; and I will be their God, and they shall be My people. They will not teach again, each one his neighbor and each one his brother, saying, 'Know the LORD,' for they will all know Me, from the least of them to the greatest of them," declares the LORD, "for I will forgive their wrongdoing, and their sin I will no longer remember."

It's as if Jesus is telling Nicodemus, "Nicodemus, don't you know that in your fallen nature, you are only prone to evil? Nicodemus, don't you remember that your heart is only wicked all the time? Nicodemus, don't you understand that your heart is deceitful and beyond cure? Nicodemus, God needs to remove your heart of stone from your flesh and give you a heart of flesh and give you a new spirit. Nicodemus, you don't perform this work, God does it. Nicodemus, don't you remember that God is the one that writes His law on your heart and mind? Nicodemus, don't you realize that when you receive this new heart and new spirit, God's laws will be written on them as well? Nicodemus, how do you earn getting a new heart and a new spirit? Nicodemus, don't you see that the old covenant was written on stone tablets and the promised new covenant will be written on the heart of flesh? Nicodemus, don't you know that it is God who must completely change your intellect, affections, and will?"

Ezekiel 36:27—The LORD says, "And I will put my Spirit in you and move you to follow my decrees and be careful to keep my laws."

As part of this new covenant promise, the LORD promises that He will put His Spirit in us to walk in His ways. So let's recap. The LORD is saying that He will forgive our sins. The LORD will cleanse us from our impurities and sins. The LORD will write His law on our heart and mind. The LORD will give us a new heart and spirit and completely change us. Finally, the LORD will give us His Spirit so that we will be careful and able to obey Him. It's God who forgives our sins. It's God who cleanses us from our sin. It's God who gives us a new heart, new spirit, and completely changes our nature and will. It's God who writes His law on our heart. It's God who writes His law on our mind. It's God who gives us a heart of flesh. It's God who puts His Spirit in us. It's God who gives a heart to fear Him. It's God who gives us the new heart to return to Him wholeheartedly." Let's say it another way. It's God who causes you to be born from above. It's God who gives you the gift of faith. It's God who gives you the gift of repentance. It's all about God monergistically saving man. Jesus is most certainly not meaning to say that being born of water and the Spirit is reference to Christian baptism. To say John 3:5 is referring to Christian baptism is to take Jesus' conversation with Nicodemus completely out of context.

John 3:6—Flesh gives birth to flesh, but the Spirit gives birth to spirit.

It's as if Jesus is telling Nicodemus that he needs to go back and study his theology of man. Jesus is telling Nicodemus to go back and study man's total depravity and inability to please God on his own merits. You can almost hear Jesus telling Nicodemus to recall the depravity of man:

- Psalm 14:2–3—The LORD has looked down from heaven upon the children of man, to see if there are any who understand, who seek after God. They have all turned aside; together they have become corrupt; there is none who does good, not even one.
- Isaiah 53:6—We all, like sheep, have gone astray, each of us has turned to our own way; and the LORD has laid on him the iniquity of us all.
- Genesis 6:5—The LORD saw how great the wickedness of the human race had become on the earth, and that every inclination of the thoughts of the human heart was only evil all the time.

- Jeremiah 17:9—The heart is deceitful above all things and beyond cure. Who can understand it?
- Psalm 51:5—Surely I was sinful at birth, sinful from the time my mother conceived me
- Ecclesiastes 7:20—Indeed, there is not a righteous man on earth who continually does good and who never sins.
- Ezekiel 37:1–2—The hand of the LORD was on me, and he brought me out by the Spirit of the LORD and set me in the middle of a valley; it was full of bones. He led me back and forth among them, and I saw a great many bones on the floor of the valley, bones that were very dry.
- Psalm 24:3–4—Who may ascend the mountain of the LORD? Who may stand in his holy place? The one who has clean hands and a pure heart, who does not trust in an idol or swear by a false god.

Jesus is telling Nicodemus that the only thing that man can produce is flesh and wickedness. Man can do nothing that produces any spiritual life. If flesh can only produce flesh, then flesh can only produce sin. Flesh can only produce spiritual death. Flesh is incapable of producing righteousness. Jesus also says that the Spirit gives birth to spirit. Once again, Nicodemus should have known what this meant, and Jesus seeks to remind him that only by the Spirit can man live. Only by the Spirit can man have spiritual life.

- Ezekiel 36:27—And I will put my Spirit in you and move you to follow my decrees and be careful to keep my laws.
- Ezekiel 37:14—I will put my Spirit in you and you will live, and I will settle you in your own land. Then you will know that I the LORD have spoken, and I have done it, declares the LORD.

- Genesis 2:7—Then the LORD God formed man of dust from the ground, and breathed into his nostrils the breath of life; and man became a living being.
- Job 33:4—The Spirit of God has made me, And the breath of the Almighty gives me life.
- Psalm 33:6—By the word of the LORD the heavens were made, and by the breath of His mouth all their host.

Judaism had reached a terrible level of legalism and rituals. Jesus shut the door to works, actions, rituals, and externality, which was emphasized by the Pharisees. Jesus declared that these things did not give you entrance into the kingdom of God. Entrance to the kingdom of God was by the regenerating work of God the Holy Spirit.

John 3:7—You should not be surprised at my saying, "You must be born again."

Jesus reiterates the same truth to Nicodemus that He stated in verse 3. In verse 3, Jesus says you must be born from above to even see the kingdom of God. In other words, you can't even see how to be reconciled with God and be saved unless you have been born from above. Jesus is saying this to Nicodemus a second time as He is emphasizing this important point to teach Nicodemus of the sovereign monergistic work of God. In fact, He tells Nicodemus, "You should not be surprised." The original language translates this word *thaumases* or *thaumazo*, which means "to wonder at, be amazed (i.e., astonished out of one's senses, awestruck), or to regard with amazement." In other words, this teaching of being born from above should not have been a new or amazing teaching.

Let's also notice in this verse that Jesus says, "You must be born again." Jesus is saying that "you" must be born from above again. There are two important words here. The first word of importance is *"you."* Here, Jesus is saying this is a personal birth from above. This is not a group birth but a personal birth, from above, that must occur. Just as you came into the world at a certain location and at a certain time, so it is with your spiritual birth. Unless a man is born from above, he will not enter or see the kingdom of God. Secondly, Jesus says, "You **must** be born again." The original word *dei* means that it is necessary. This second birth is a necessity. Without a second birth, you have no spiritual life. Without a second birth, you are dead in trespasses, alienated from God, and an enemy of the Lord. Jesus is emphasizing the importance and necessity of the new birth to enter the kingdom of God.

John 3:8—The wind blows wherever it pleases. You hear its sound, but you cannot tell where it comes from or where it is going. So it is with everyone born of the Spirit.

If we are closely following along to Jesus, we see that He is saying you must be born from above which is something that God controls and not man (v. 3). Jesus is saying that we must be born of water and the Spirit which is in reference to Ezekiel 36, where God is sovereignly acting to give man a new heart, a new spirit, and put His Spirit within man (v. 5). He has stated that man in his depraved state can only produce flesh and sin, but the Spirit gives birth to spirit and life (v. 6). Jesus states again the necessity of being born from above to Nicodemus (v. 7). Thus far, we have Jesus making four statements that man's entrance into the kingdom of God is a work from God the Holy Spirit where the Holy Spirit monergistically acts to change man and give him spiritual life. Jesus is going to give another earthly analogy to explain a spiritual reality. This time, He chooses the wind as a metaphor. Jesus' first statement is that the wind blows where it pleases. This is to draw Nicodemus to the following understanding:

- What can you do to start the wind?
- What can you do to stop the wind?
- What can you do to influence the wind?
- What can you do to control the wind?

The answer to these questions is nothing. Just as man cannot control the wind, so man cannot control the Spirit. There is nothing done by man to influence the wind. There is nothing done by man to control the wind. There is nothing done by man to command the wind. The Spirit operates freely and totally by Divine will. This is Jesus' point.

The second point Jesus makes with the wind metaphor is that you can hear its sound, but you cannot tell where it comes from or where it is going. So, it is with everyone born of the Spirit. Here Jesus is saying that when the Spirit operates, you hear His sound. Another way of restating this is, when the Spirit operates, you will know that there was a work done by the Spirit. When the Spirit operates, it will be obvious that a work of God was done to change a man. When the Spirit operates, you will see a man with a new nature and new affections. You will not know where the Spirit came from or went, but it will be obvious that someone was operated on by the Spirit. Jesus' analogy of the way the wind works being analogous to the Spirit cannot be mistaken. He is emphasizing the monergistic work of God and the transformational outcome. We can't control the wind or the Spirit, but we will be able to tell when the Spirit has been at work. Just like we can't control a tornado or a hurricane, we will see when there has been a tornado or a hurricane and we will see the evidence of it. Everyone born of the Spirit has undergone a sovereign monergistic work of God the Holy Spirit and, where God the Holy Spirit has acted, it will be clear that there will be a person with a new heart, new spirit, and the Spirit of God working in that person.

John 3:9–10—"How can this be?" Nicodemus asked. "You are Israel's teacher," said Jesus, "and do you not understand these things?"

Nicodemus has still not understood the meaning of the second birth and Jesus is unveiling the spiritual depth to which Israel and one of Israel's premier teachers has fallen. A better translation of "You are Israel's teacher" could be as follows, "You are **the** teacher of Israel and these things you do not know?" This is a definite article. Jesus is not saying you are ***a*** teacher, but ***the*** teacher. In other words, Nicodemus is the premier teacher of Judaism in Israel, and he has not grasped the understanding of the new birth and God's Spirit bringing life to spiritually dead men. Nicodemus should have known the new covenant promise in Ezekiel 36. Nicodemus should have known the new covenant promise in Jeremiah 33 where God writes His laws on man's heart and mind. Nicodemus should have known total depravity. Nicodemus should have known that man's good works are like filthy rags. Nicodemus should have known that man can't give himself spiritual life. Jesus is telling "the" teacher in Israel that he needs to start all over because he doesn't understand the sovereign saving work of God and needs to start over and be born from above to enter the kingdom of God. Jesus is telling Nicodemus that salvation has always been from God and not from man. How far Israel had fallen. No wonder Jesus was moved with compassion in Matthew 9:36 as He saw that His covenant people were harassed and helpless, like sheep without a shepherd.

In covering John 3:1–10, we can understand the doctrine of regeneration according to Jesus. From this text, we can take away the following understanding of the doctrine of regeneration.

- Man cannot see the kingdom of God unless he is born from above. (v. 3)
- Man cannot repent of sins or come to saving faith unless he is born from above. (v. 3)
- Man cannot see or understand how to be saved unless he is born from above. (v. 3)
    - John 1:13—children born not of natural descent, nor of human decision or a husband's will, but born of God
- *Regeneration* is a monergistic act on God the Holy Spirit's behalf to change the nature and character of man. (v. 5)

- ○ 1 Peter 1:3—Praise be to the God and Father of our Lord Jesus Christ! In his great mercy, he has given us new birth into a living hope through the resurrection of Jesus Christ from the dead.
- ○ 1 Peter 1:23—For you have been born again, not of perishable seed, but of imperishable, through the living and enduring word of God.

- Man is spiritually dead and cannot save himself. (v. 6)
- The Holy Spirit gives spiritual life to spiritually dead men. (v. 6)
- Being born from above or regenerated is necessary for salvation to take place. (v. 7).
- Being born from above is a one-time event just as an earthly birth is a one-time event. (v. 7)
- The Holy Spirit cannot be controlled, coerced, or commanded by man. (v. 8)
- Evidence of the Holy Spirit's work can be seen in man. (v. 8)
- Regeneration is not Christian baptism. (John 3:1–10)

CHAPTER 2

John the Baptist's Baptism of Repentance for the Forgiveness of Sins

Luke 3:7–8 John said to the crowds coming out to be baptized by him, "You brood of vipers! Who warned you to flee from the coming wrath? Produce fruit in keeping with repentance. And do not begin to say to yourselves, 'We have Abraham as our father.' For I tell you that out of these stones God can raise up children for Abraham."

John the Baptist had an extraordinary ministry. John the Baptist was the son of a priest named Zechariah who belonged to the priestly division of Abijah. John's mother was Elizabeth, who was also a descendant of Aaron. Elizabeth was related to Mary, the mother of Jesus, so John the Baptist would have also been related to Jesus. John was the forerunner to Jesus and had the ministry of getting the nation of Israel ready for the Messiah and preparing the way of the Lord. John's ministry was to bring back many of the people of Israel to the Lord their God and to turn the hearts of the parents to their children and the disobedient to the wisdom of the righteous—to make ready a people prepared for the Lord (Luke 1:17). John was to go before the Lord in the spirit and power of Elijah, which means he would be known for being bold and uncompromising in his stand for the Word of God (Luke 1:17). It is important to look at John's baptism of repentance to fully understand its purpose and to help understand the difference between baptism of repentance for the forgiveness of sins and Baptism with the Holy Spirit and understand that the baptism or ritual that John performed was not what gave forgiveness of sins. Additionally, understanding John the Baptist's baptism of repentance will also help us develop a definition of *repentance*. Although we will further define *repentance* in this chapter, it is good to have a starting definition of *repentance,* which is: ***Repentance*** **is a gift from God where the sinner understands his sin against God (intellect), has Godly sorrow and mourns over his sin against God (emotions and affections), and turns away from his sin and towards God for righteousness (will or volition).**

To do this, let's look at John's baptism of repentance in Luke 3.

Luke 3:3—He went into all the country around the Jordan, preaching a baptism of repentance for the forgiveness of sins.

John begins his ministry preaching a baptism of repentance. Let's stop and pause to understand "preached a baptism of repentance." The first word to observe is *preached. Preached* is translated from *kérussó* which means "to herald, to proclaim, and to preach a message publicly and with conviction and persuasion." The second word to understand is *repentance.* In the original language, the word is *metanoia. Metanoia* means "a change of mind." This changing of the mind is not mere intellectual assent, but also impacts the emotional affections and the volitional will of man. A good definition of *repentance* would be a combination of 2 Corinthians 7:10 and Matthew 5:3–6. In 2 Corinthians 7:10, it says:

"For the sorrow that is according to the will of God produces a repentance without regret, leading to salvation, but the sorrow of the world produces death." Matthew 5:3–6, along with the explanation to these verses, will further help us develop our understanding of repentance:

- Matthew 5:3—Blessed are the poor in spirit, for theirs is the kingdom of heaven.
    - *Ptóchos* has been translated to "poor," but it means beggarly poor of one who crouches and cowers because all he can do is hold out his hand. It is the extreme opposite of rich. In other words, Jesus is saying, blessed are those who are so spiritually bankrupt in their spirit and realize they have no right standing before God. Blessed are those who are so troubled and anguished in their spirit that all they can do is crouch and ask for mercy from God. These people are blessed for theirs is the kingdom of God. Isaiah 57:15 is another excellent cross-reference for poor in spirit where the LORD says, "I live in a high and holy place, but also with the one who is contrite and lowly in spirit, to revive the spirit of the lowly and to revive the heart of the contrite." Isaiah 66:2 is an excellent cross-reference that talks about the poor in spirit where the LORD says, "These are the ones I look on with favor: those who are humble and contrite in spirit, and who tremble at my word."
- Matthew 5:4—Blessed are those who mourn, for they will be comforted.
    - *Pentheó* has been translated "mourn" and it means mourning as if grieving over a death. This mourning is so severe that it takes possession of a person and cannot be hidden. This is not talking about those who mourn over losing a job or a loved one. It cannot mean that because even people in false religions mourn over such

things. No, Jesus is saying that those who mourn, weep, and wail over their own personal sins against God have divine favor. Those who will mourn over how they have sinned against God will be comforted. Those who will say the same thing about their sin as what God says about sin will be comforted by God. Joel 2:12–13 is an excellent cross-reference for mourning over sin, "'Even now,' declares the LORD, 'return to me with all your heart, with fasting and weeping and mourning.' Rend your heart and not your garments. Return to the LORD your GOD, for he is gracious and compassionate, slow to anger and abounding in love, and he relents from sending calamity."

- Matthew 5:5—Blessed are the meek for they shall inherit the earth.
  - First, the word *meekness* does not mean weakness. No, this word carries with it the idea of submission unto a master. It could also be thought of as strength under control. This is a person who will no longer exercise untamed power and control but will submit to a master. This word was used to describe breaking in a horse. Before breaking in a horse, the horse would buck, bite, and kick, but after the horse had been broken in and the bit and bridle put into its mouth, it would be considered "meeked." This is not to say the horse lost its power, but rather, the power remained and was directed by its master. So it is with those who enter the kingdom. They come in submission to God. They are meeked because of their sin and submit to the Lord Jesus Christ. Those who are meek shall inherit the earth. Those who are meek because of their sin and submit to the authority of Jesus Christ shall inherit "a new heaven and a new earth" (Revelation 21:1).

- Matthew 5:6—Blessed are those who hunger and thirst for righteousness, for they will be satisfied.
  - Thinking of hunger and thirsting is hard in the United States or in First World countries. Most people have never experienced this in their lives. However, for those who have been so hungry where they have no strength, have body aches, and body pains, they would know what this means. Likewise, those who are so deprived of water where they have dryness of throat, where they have no strength, and where they experience dehydration would know of this thirsting. Jesus is saying those who hunger and thirst for righteousness in such a way have divine favor from God. In other words, those who hunger and thirst for the righteousness that can only be found in Jesus Christ will be satisfied. Not only will they hunger and thirst for the righteousness of Christ for their justification before God, they will also be hungering and thirsting for more righteousness to be conformed to the image of the Son of God.

True repentance will be sorrowful over sinning against God, will know of the spiritual bankruptcy before God, will deeply mourn over sinning against God, will be meek, gentle, and submissive towards God, and will turn to Christ for righteousness and turn away from sin. True repentance is also a gift. Acts 5:31 says, "He is the one whom God exalted to His right hand as a Prince and a Savior, to grant repentance to Israel, and forgiveness of sins." In 2 Timothy 2:24–25, it says, "The Lord's bond-servant must not be quarrelsome, but be kind to all, skillful in teaching, patient when wronged, with gentleness correcting those who are in opposition, if perhaps God may grant them repentance leading to the knowledge of the truth." Acts 11:18 says, "When they heard this they quieted down and glorified God, saying, "Well then, God has also granted to the Gentiles the repentance that leads to life." If there is just sorrow over sin but no turning from the sin towards God, this is *a false repentance*. If there is sorrow over sin and a turning from the sin but no turning to God, this is mere *moral reform* and not true repentance (Matt 12:43-45). Thus, a proper definition of *repentance* can be as follows: ***Repentance* is a gift from God where the sinner understands his sin against God (intellect), has Godly sorrow and mourns over his sin against God (emotions and affections), and turns away from his sin and towards God for righteousness (will or volition)**. Understanding genuine repentance is important. When preaching repentance, it must be understood that it includes Godly sorrow, turning away from sin, and turning to God for righteousness. Additionally, repentance must be understood as a gift from God. Otherwise, repentance could be understood as someone working for one's salvation through repentance. True repentance is a gift from God.

John's ministry was one of confrontation with the nation of Israel. It was not only a call to national repentance, but also a call to personal repentance. In ancient times, the herald would go before a king and announce the king's message. The herald would come with the king's message and whether it was an order for the nation's surrender or an edict from the king, the messenger would go throughout the towns and villages and announce the king's message. The herald would not be quiet. The herald would bring forth the message with conviction and all authority of the king. The herald would neither dare to misrepresent the king's message nor would the herald quietly announce the message. The herald would boldly, loudly, and clearly articulate with conviction the message of the king to all people. John the Baptist was no different. His job was to boldly, loudly, and clearly articulate with conviction the message of the Lord to repent and be baptized. His message was not just a mere change of mind, but a call to prepare one's heart and life to turn away from sin and towards the Messiah. His message was that all of Israel needed to repent and be baptized for the forgiveness of sins. So, the next question that arises is what did this baptism represent?

There were several ceremonial washings in the Old Testament. However, there was a specific meaning behind John's baptism that would have been especially offensive. Under the old covenant, there was a ceremonial ablution for Gentiles who would convert to Judaism. Bathing of proselytes was considered purification from heathenism and an initiation or consecration of the convert before his admission to the people of God. Furthermore, since a Gentile had lived in what was considered heathen pollution, and was also considered a heathen and impure, the Gentile would be required to complete a purification process to fully become an Israelite. It was, thus, required of every Gentile to submit to the rite of purification from heathen pollution by immersion. The Babylonian Talmud says concerning proselytes that "one is not to be regarded as a proselyte until he has been circumcised and undergone immersion, and as long as he has not undergone immersion, he is still a non-Jew." This was a part of rabbinical regulations for ceremonial purifications and required three witnesses. The candidate, if a male, was first circumcised and when the wound had healed, he was taken to the bath. While he stood in the water, the Rabbis once more recited to him some of the great and lesser commandments. Then the convert made a complete immersion and stepped forth as a fully privileged Israelite." In addition to this, the proselyte would be asked questions such as, "What makes thee desire to become a proselyte?" and if the proselyte would answer, "I am not worthy to give my neck to the yoke of Him who spoke the word and the world came into existence," they would immediately accept him and move forward with the baptism while also reciting commandments.

John's baptism of repentance was a proselyte baptism of repentance for Israel. In other words, John was proclaiming to them loudly, boldly, clearly, and with conviction that they were not ready for the Messiah. John was telling them that they needed to see themselves as Gentiles. John was telling them that their circumcision meant nothing in terms of salvation. John was telling them that their ancestry meant nothing in terms of salvation. John was telling them that their religious rituals meant nothing in terms of salvation. John was telling them that their good works meant nothing in terms of salvation. John was telling them that they were not ready for the Messiah and, if they wanted to receive forgiveness of sins that could be offered by the Messiah, they would need to consider themselves as Gentiles. John was telling them that if they wanted forgiveness of sins as offered by the Messiah, they should consider themselves outside of God's covenant people, that they should consider themselves cut off from God, that they should consider themselves ceremonially unclean to accept the Messiah, that they should consider themselves as equals with the Gentile pagan, and that they should consider themselves unrighteous and damned. This was John's baptism for the forgiveness of sins.

It would have been an extreme shock to the Jews who thought they were the covenant people and righteous. This message would have turned their world upside down as John not only commanded all of Israel to repent and identify as a Gentile, but even the religious leaders of Judaism. No one in the nation of Israel was excluded from the command to be baptized, repent, identify as a Gentile, confess their sins, and throw themselves at the mercy of the Messiah. This was an extreme message for the Jews to prepare for the Messiah's coming and it was a radical call to turn not only nationally, but also personally to the Messiah. Isaiah 1:5–6 captures the state of where Israel was just prior to the Messiah's coming, "Why should you be beaten anymore? Why do you persist in rebellion? Your whole head is injured, your whole heart afflicted. From the sole of your foot to the top of your head there is no soundness—only wounds and welts and open sores, not cleansed or bandaged or soothed with olive oil." John proclaimed this same message.

Luke 3:4-6—As it is written in the book of the words of Isaiah the prophet: "A voice of one calling in the wilderness, 'Prepare the way for the Lord, make straight paths for him. Every valley shall be filled in, every mountain and hill made low. The crooked roads shall become straight, the rough ways smooth. And all people will see God's salvation.'"

John the Baptist has just quoted from Isaiah 40. Although the message and baptism of repentance would have been shocking and offensive as it called for a radical spiritual repentance, John was also referencing a promise from Isaiah where God comforts His people. In Isaiah 40, God announces comfort for His people (v. 1), God has said that Jerusalem's penalty has been paid for twice over (v. 2), God promises to tend to His flock like a shepherd (v. 11), God declares His sovereignty and power (v. 15–25), and promises hope for those who trust in Him (29–31). John is preparing Israel to receive their Messiah and he begins to explain repentance through Isaiah 40:3–5.

John's theology of repentance according to Isaiah starts with "Prepare the way for the Lord, make straight paths for him." In this short little sentence, John is saying that any obstacles that would deter men from accepting the Messiah must be put away. John is saying that every person needs to clean out their spiritual closet. He is saying that everyone in Israel needs to get rid of their apathy, get rid of their pride, get rid of their distractions, get rid of false religion, get rid of other priorities that interfere with God, get rid of self-reliance, get rid of hypocrisy, and get rid of anything that is going to prevent you from accepting the Messiah.

He goes on to state that the crooked roads shall become straight, the rough ways smooth. John was calling for a total self-evaluation. In verse 5, he said, "Every valley shall be filled in, every mountain and hill made low." When John said that "every valley shall be filled in," he was stating that every sin shall be brought up and openly confessed. Take your sins and confess them and do not hold anything back. All the debase sins that you cherish shall be raised up and elevated so that you may be brought low and humbled to receive the Messiah. Notice that he says "every." This was a radical repentance. He was saying that the sins that the people knew about in their lives needed to be confessed and rejected. He was saying that all the hidden sins in the valley of one's heart needed to be exposed. Likewise, John said that "every mountain and hill needed to be brought low." He's stating that every righteous act and that every self-exalting accomplishment must be brought low. He's saying that your sins must be elevated, all your good deeds and religious accomplishments brought low, and every other obstacle in your life must be dealt with and removed.

Luke 3:7–8—John said to the crowds coming out to be baptized by him, "You, brood of vipers! Who warned you to flee from the coming wrath? Produce fruit in keeping with repentance. And do not begin to say to yourselves, 'We have Abraham as our father.' For I tell you that out of these stones God can raise up children for Abraham."

So, as John is performing his ministry of preparing the nation of Israel for the Messiah, he is also confronting people that do not have true repentance. Here, he calls them "a brood of vipers." Notice that he doesn't call them "Abraham's descendants." He doesn't call them "children of God." He doesn't call them "sons of Israel." No, he calls them a *brood of vipers* or in the original language *gennemata,* which can also be translated as "offspring or child." He is calling them "children of serpents." In Matthew's account, he is speaking specifically with Sadducees and Pharisees, but, in Luke's account, Luke makes no distinction and includes the crowds. He is not calling them "covenant people of God," but "children of the devil." He is warning them of divine wrath and judgment. The people of Israel would have picked up on this. They would have known of the serpent in Genesis 3. They would have known that John was telling them they were still under divine wrath and judgment. Notice too that he tells this to the crowds. Israel should have known better that entrance into the kingdom was not a group affair but an individual entrance into the kingdom. They would have known Psalm 1:1–2, "Blessed is the one who does not walk in step with the wicked or stand in the way of sinners or sit in the seat of scoffers, but whose delight is in the law of the LORD, and who meditates on His law day and night." They would have known that this should have been an individual repentance and not just another ritual to go through.

Notice as well that he says, "Who warned you to flee from the coming wrath?" In other words, John is saying, "So you heard that there was a baptism of repentance and now you're looking to go through a ceremonial rite or ritual. Don't do that! Don't think that divine judgment will not fall on you just because you've been baptized. Don't presume that the Jordan River will make you right with God." John further goes on to clarify repentance when he says, "Produce fruit in keeping with repentance." There's an interesting word that is used in the original language which is *axios* and it can also mean "worthy, worthy of, deserving, or suitable." Another way of describing *axios* is to "weigh in, assigning the matching value or worth-to-worth (i.e. as the assessment in keeping with how something "weighs in" on God's balance-scale of truth)." In other words, John is telling them that this ritual means nothing, but what means everything is the heart preparation as it relates to repentance. If the people of Israel do see their offense towards God, have intellectual knowledge of their sins, understand they have no merit before God, mourn over their status before God, and humble themselves to obey God and receive the Messiah, they should bring forth fruit that God finds worthy of repentance. If there is no fruit, there was never a root of true repentance, but rather, a false repentance and dead ritual. This not only applies to the people of Israel, but this applies to all people today. God commands all men everywhere to repent (Acts 17:30).

John was very concerned about false repentance. John knew how wicked the heart was and how man would want the easy road. John knew that not everyone who came to be baptized for repentance would bear fruits of repentance. John was preparing the people for the Messiah and was trying to warn them of a repentance that bore no true fruit. A repentance that bears no fruit is a *dead repentance*. A repentance that doesn't elevate the sins is a *dead repentance*. A repentance that doesn't bring one's pride and righteous accomplishments down low is a *dead repentance*. A repentance that does no soul searching to remove spiritual obstacles from the heart is a *dead repentance*.

In verse 8 he says, "And do not begin to say to yourselves, 'We have Abraham as our father.' For I tell you that out of these stones God can raise up children for Abraham." John is making quite a statement here. He knows that the Jews are inclined to say they are the covenant children of God based on their national heritage. He knows that they are going to say they are circumcised and have the covenant sign. He knows that they are going to say they have the law of Moses, the Levitical system, and more. However, John is telling them not to presume you are righteous just because of your affiliation. Don't presume that because you're a born Israelite that you have right standing with God. Don't presume to say that because you're a priest and have been circumcised that you are eternally blessed by God. Likewise, John's message bears weight today. Today's message to the church would be to say, "Don't presume because you've had a Christian baptism that you're going to heaven. Don't presume because you've made a profession of faith that you have eternal life or the Son. Don't presume because you've gone through confirmation that you have saving faith. Don't presume that because you're a part of a church that teaches biblical and orthodox doctrine that you are in the kingdom of God. No. Rather, you "need to produce fruit worthy of repentance."

Additionally, in verse 8, he says God is able from these stones to raise up children for Abraham. Once again, this was a hard and demeaning message. He has just gotten done calling them snakes and now he is saying that their position is no better than dirt. Once again, he's not calling them God's covenant people, but he's saying that God can raise up dirt from the ground to be sons of Abraham. No doubt that this would have been incredibly offensive to the nation of Israel, but John's message of repentance was radical and demanded the people's heart be prepared for the Messiah.

Luke 3:9—The ax is already at the root of the trees, and every tree that does not produce good fruit will be cut down and thrown into the fire.

John is exhorting the Israelites to earnestly repent, but there is another element to repentance. Notice that John says, "The ax is already at the root of the trees." He is speaking of the urgency of needing to repent. The Israelites would have known what it meant for *the ax to be at the root of the tree*. This means that the one who is chopping down the tree only has one more swing of the ax before the tree falls. His ax has chopped away the bark and made it through the pulp and now there's only one more swing that will complete the fall of the tree. John was speaking of the urgency to repent. Not only had he clarified the nature of repentance, but now he was emphasizing the urgency of repentance. Don't wait one more day. Don't put this off. As John had referenced Isaiah 40, surely the people would have also remembered Isaiah 40:6–8, "All people are like grass, and all their faithfulness is like the flowers of the field. The grass withers and the flowers fall, because the breath of the LORD blows on them. Surely the people are grass. The grass withers and the flowers fall, but the word of our God endures forever." Surely, they would have known that time was of the essence in repentance. Jesus had also emphasized the point of urgently repenting when in Luke 13:6–9 He gives a parable of a fig tree that has been given care for three years but has shown no fruit. While the man who was growing the fig tree was patient for three years, He gave it one more year to bear fruit otherwise He would cut it down. So, it is today that we must exhort men to repent. We can ascend no higher than John. We have no better message than what John, Jesus, or the apostles said. All men must repent and bear fruit worthy of repentance for their time on earth is short.

The next point John brings up is that a man that bears no fruit of repentance is not saved. The man that says he believes but produces no good fruit is an unbeliever and is unsaved. The destiny of a man who bears no fruit is evidence that the man was never regenerated. It is evidence that this man never had saving faith. The end of this man is an eternal punishment of fire in hell. Let's also stop and pause to note that John says "every" tree that does not produce good fruit is cut down. There is no exception to this. Either a man bears fruits of repentance or he doesn't.

Lastly, let us see that this fire is an unquenchable fire. In verse 17, He says that His winnowing fork is in His hand to clear His threshing floor and to gather the wheat into His barn, but He will burn up the chaff with unquenchable fire. Once again, John is saying that time is of the essence. The farmer is separating the wheat and the chaff. The wheat has already been harvested. It's no longer growing season, but it is now a time of separation. The wheat is brought into the barn which refers to believers, but the chaff, which represents unbelievers, is burned up with unquenchable fire. In those days, the people would have known what John was talking about with "burning the chaff with unquenchable fire." They lived in an agricultural community. The people would have known that when you burn chaff the fire will eventually subside as it runs out of substrate and is quenched. However, John's theology on hell and eternal punishment lines right up with Jesus' theology on hell. Note that John says that the chaff will be burned up with unquenchable fire. This fire that John was referring to was an eternal fire. There's no mistaking it.

This was a fire that would not go out once it had consumed the chaff. No, this fire would persist forever. This fire would not go out. The fire would never be quenched. The chaff would never stop burning. A man that bears no fruit of repentance is on his way to an unquenchable fire that will never go out. Let us etch this in our minds that the Gospel contains many elements, but it must always include divine wrath, divine judgment, and repentance. Often, we are too quick to say, "Put your faith in Jesus Christ and you will be saved." However, let us learn from John that although the Gospel also includes an explanation of the person and work of Christ as well as the subjective elements of human response (i.e., faith), we must not leave out divine wrath, divine judgment, and repentance as we warn men and call them to Jesus Christ.

Luke 3:10–11—"What should we do then?" the crowd asked. John answered, "Anyone who has two shirts should share with the one who has none, and anyone who has food should do the same."

John continues to expound on his theology of repentance. Notice that John notes what true repentance will look like on the horizontal level or, rather, towards man. True repentance will love your neighbor as yourself. John would certainly have in mind Leviticus 19:18, "Do not seek revenge or bear a grudge against anyone among our people but love your neighbor as yourself. I am the LORD." John is saying that true repentance will show itself in loving your neighbor and meeting your neighbor's needs. He explains that there is not only a negative side to repentance, which is turning away from sin, but also a positive side to repentance, which is turning to righteousness, that shows itself in acts of love that the LORD commands. Likewise, the book of James describes a faith that saves and a faith that does not save. James describes a faith that has no care of meeting a neighbor's needs and concludes that a faith that cares nothing for his neighbor and cannot meet his neighbor's essential needs is a *dead faith*.

Also, notice in verse 10 that the crowd says, "What should we do then?" Perhaps this was an honest question. Perhaps the crowd was indeed earnest to know what they needed to do. However, one ominous note here is that they needed to ask what to do rather than being deeply convicted. Perhaps they were asking out of deep conviction, but perhaps they really had no conviction at all and were blind to their sins. The main point is that if your sins are brought up to you, confess them, ask for forgiveness, ask for God's help to deliver you from the sin, and repent.

Luke 3:12–14—Even tax collectors came to be baptized. "Teacher," they asked, "what should we do?" "Don't collect any more than you are required to," he told them. Then some soldiers asked him, "And what should we do?" He replied, "Don't extort money and don't accuse people falsely—be content with your pay."

Here, John is expounding even more on true repentance. Here John tells the tax collectors to be honest in their work and stop stealing. He tells soldiers not to steal and slander. John is talking about the negative side of repentance which is the aspect of turning from sin. This is further highlighting Leviticus 19:18, which calls us to love our neighbor as ourselves. If we keep this command, we will not only positively love them by doing good to them, but we will also react in a negative sense where we will stop sinning against our neighbor. Not only this, but look at the flow of John's theology of repentance. He first explains that there is divine judgment and wrath coming in verses 7–9, which could be considered a vertical repentance towards God, but then also talks about a horizontal aspect of repentance toward men. This is how we must present repentance to all men. We must warn men of the wrath of God that is coming. We must warn men that they must turn from their sin and turn to Christ in faith for salvation. We should also explain that all men must turn from their personal sin against God, but also sinning against man. John's theology on baptism of repentance for the forgiveness of sins was thorough and complete.

In John's baptism of repentance for the forgiveness of sins, it would be a colossal mistake to think that the ritual of baptism is what forgave sins. John's message of repentance was radical, and John even warned against treating this baptism of repentance as just another ritual or ceremony. John was calling for heart-searching repentance that would bear fruit. If there was no fruit of repentance, but only a baptism, John would have warned that the person who went through the baptism was chaff that was just waiting to be burned with unquenchable fire. A person that desired to confess and reject his sins, reject his spiritual accomplishments, and get rid of the barriers of the heart in preparation for the Messiah would have been characterized as wheat according to John. Understanding repentance will be a key biblical doctrine later as we will discuss saving faith later in the book.

Chapter 3

John the Baptist's, Matthew's, Mark's, Luke's, and the Apostle John's Theology on Who Baptizes with Water and Who Baptizes with the Holy Spirit

Luke 3:15–17—The people were waiting expectantly and were all wondering in their hearts if John might possibly be the Messiah. John answered them all, "I baptize you with water. But one who is more powerful than I will come, the straps of whose sandals I am not worthy to untie. He will baptize you with the Holy Spirit and fire."

In the previous section, we examined John's baptism of repentance for the forgiveness of sins. We understood that the water is not what forgave sins. Rather, John was heralding a heartfelt repentance that brought up the debase sin in one's life, that brought one's pride and spiritual achievements down low, and that cleared out the spiritual obstacles and distractions of one's heart to prepare for receiving the Messiah. We also saw that this baptism of repentance was an offensive Gentile, proselyte baptism that made the people of Israel acknowledge they were no better than Gentiles. We also saw that, with this baptism of repentance, John had to warn the people not to treat this like another ritual or rite which would have been a false repentance. We saw that true repentance will ultimately lead to faith in Christ the Messiah. Lastly, we came to an understanding of biblical repentance which could be captured in the following definition: ***Repentance*** **is a gift from God where the sinner understands his sin against God (intellect), has Godly sorrow and mourns over his sin against God (emotions and affections), and turns away from his sin and towards God for righteousness (will or volition).**

The doctrine of baptism with the Holy Spirit is certainly a controversial doctrine. In fact, baptism in general can be hard to understand as there are certain texts in the Bible where it could be difficult to discern if the baptism is one of water or a baptism with the Holy Spirit. Often, the context in which baptism is used will help to determine the meaning. Regarding baptism with the Holy Spirit, some Christian denominations may tend to teach that this is a secondary work of God, others may say this is a one-time act of God whereby He saves sinners. I don't think this book will solve the issue. However, Scripture is adequate to demonstrate what baptism with the Holy Spirit is and to draw distinctions between water baptism and baptism with the Holy Spirit. We will go into greater depth as to what baptism with the Holy Spirit is in chapter 4 and subsequent chapters as there are several passages that help us understand the baptism with the Holy Spirit. However, for the purposes of this chapter, it is helpful to use the following definition for *baptism with the Holy Spirit*: **The baptism with the Holy Spirit is the sovereign monergistic work of salvation performed by God the Father, God the Son, and God the Holy Spirit. The Holy Spirit is given from the Father to**

the Son (John 14:16, 15:26, Luke 11:13) and the Son pours out or gives the Holy Spirit in the Father's name (Matthew 3:11-12, Mark 1:8, Luke 3:16, 24:49 John 1:31-33, 14:16, 14:26, 15:26, 16:7; Acts 1:4-5, 2:17-18, 10:44-48, 11:16, Titus 3:6). The Holy Spirit then regenerates or causes man to be born again (John 3:3-10, Titus 3:5, Ezekiel 36:25-27) through hearing the Word of God/Gospel (James 1:18, Ephesians 1:13, Romans 1:15-17, 10:17, 1 Corinthians 1:21) which gives spiritual life to the previously spiritually dead man (Ephesians 2:1-3, Colossians 2:13). God then grants man the ability to repent which is a gift (Acts 11:18, 2 Timothy 2:25) and put saving faith in Jesus Christ which is also a gift (Ephesians 2:8-9, Philippians 1:29, John 7:38-39). Man is then justified by grace through faith in Christ (Titus 3:7), receives and is indwelt by the Holy Spirit (Galatians 3:2, 3:14, Ephesians 1:13, 1 Corinthians 6:19), and the Holy Spirit spiritually unites/immerses man with Jesus Christ and puts the man into the body of Christ (1 Corinthians 12:13, Romans 6:3-4). The baptism with the Holy Spirit is not water baptism and water baptism is not the baptism with the Holy Spirit for only Christ can baptize with the Holy Spirit and man can only baptize with water (Matthew 3:11-12, Mark 1:8, Luke 3:16, John 1:31-33, 3:8, 7:38-39, 14:15-17, 14:26, 15:26, 16:7; Acts 1:4-5, 2:17-18, 10:44-48, 11:16, 1 Corinthians 1:17). The baptism with the Holy Spirit is a one-time, instantaneous, and salvific work of God (1 Corinthians 12:13). This chapter is not set out to define *baptism with the Holy Spirit* as the subsequent chapters will fill in and enrich the different facets of this definition, but rather to define who baptizes with the Holy Spirit and who does not baptize with the Holy Spirit. Lastly, this chapter will show that a prophet, the apostles, and Jesus Christ knew there was a difference between water baptism and baptism with the Holy Spirit.

Luke 3:15–17—The people were waiting expectantly and were all wondering in their hearts if John might possibly be the

Messiah. John answered them all, "I baptize you with water. But one who is more powerful than I will come, the straps of whose sandals I am not worthy to untie. He will baptize you with the Holy Spirit and fire."

After John's explanation of repentance, he makes an incredible statement about baptism that must be remembered. As the people were wondering if John may be the Messiah, he launches into his theology on who baptizes with the Holy Spirit where he says, "I baptize you with water. But one who is more powerful than I will come, the straps of whose sandals I am not worthy to untie. He will baptize you with the Holy Spirit and fire." What a powerful statement. John is essentially saying, "Israel, I am just a man. I can only baptize you with water. Likewise, every man after me can only baptize with water. However, the Christ will baptize you with the Holy Spirit and fire. I can't baptize you with the Holy Spirit. I can't baptize you with fire. No man after me can baptize with the Holy Spirit and fire except for the Christ." John has just shut the door on baptismal regeneration through water baptism. John has put an exclamation point on water baptism's efficacy to save. John, being inspired by the Holy Spirit, has just pronounced that only the Christ can baptize with the Holy Spirit and fire. Let us sear this to our memory. Let us hold this fast in our hearts. Let us not forget who the author and pioneer of our faith is. No man pouring water on us or immersing us can give us saving faith. No ritual can save us. No rite or sacrament can save us. John knew nothing of the word being connected with the water. John knew nothing of the word and command being in, with, and under the water to make baptism a life-giving ritual. John knew nothing about the Holy Spirit being given in water baptism. John had it exactly right. Man is man and can only baptize with water.

John's baptism with the Holy Spirit and with fire does require some explanation. In verse 17, he says, "His winnowing fork is in his hand to clear his threshing floor and to gather the wheat into his barn, but He will burn up the chaff with unquenchable fire." As we mentioned earlier, John is saying that the time of tilling, planting, growing, and harvesting is already done. The farmer has the wheat on his threshing floor. The farmer is throwing the wheat and chaff in the air to separate the two components. The chaff, which is lighter, will blow away and the wheat will fall in the same place. The separation is already occurring. Although there is debate over what *baptize with the Holy Spirit and fire* means, it is helpful to understand this verse in context. In context, to be baptized with the Holy Spirit seems to indicate that this baptism ultimately ends in salvation and would most likely refer to the wheat that is brought into the barn. On the other hand, the baptism of fire seems to be tied to the chaff as the chaff is ultimately burned up with fire, thus *baptism of fire*. In other words, you are either baptized with the Holy Spirit and saved or baptized with fire and judged unto condemnation. This explanation seems to be the best fit to what John is talking about as only Jesus can baptize with the Holy Spirit and save man and He alone can judge men and send them to hell.

Let us also note that John is considered the last Old Testament prophet. So, here we see that an Old Testament prophet spoke forth the Word of God saying that man cannot baptize with the Holy Spirit. Man could only baptize with water. Jesus was the only one who could baptize with the Holy Spirit and fire.

Matthew's Theology on Who Baptizes with Water and Who Baptizes with the Holy Spirit

Matthew 3:11–12— "I baptize you with water for repentance. But after me comes one who is more powerful than I, whose sandals I am not worthy to carry. He will baptize you with the Holy Spirit and fire. His winnowing fork is in His hand, and He will clear His threshing floor and gather His wheat into the barn, but the chaff He will burn with unquenchable fire."

The apostle Matthew, also known as Levi, was a tax collector who left everything to follow Christ. Matthew's gospel has been noted as having a strong Jewish flavor by scholars. Evidence includes the opening genealogy of Matthew tracing Christ's lineage only to Abraham. Matthew also focuses on Christ as the King and Messiah of Israel. Matthew's gospel also quotes more than sixty times from Old Testament prophetic passages, emphasizing how Christ is the fulfillment of all the Old Testament promises. Matthew usually cites Jewish custom without explaining it, in contrast to other gospels. He constantly refers to Christ as the "Son of David." Matthew even guards Jewish sensibilities regarding the name of God, referring to "the kingdom of heaven" where the other evangelists speak of "the kingdom of God."

The apostle Matthew, being inspired by the Holy Spirit, noted that John the Baptist could only baptize with water, but the one who came after him, Jesus, was the one who would baptize with the Holy Spirit (salvation) and fire (judgment). Matthew spoke the same thing as John the Baptist and agreed with him wholeheartedly. Matthew penned in Scripture that man could only baptize with water. Man cannot baptize with the Holy Spirit.

Let us not forget that the apostle Matthew spent three years with the Lord and came to the same understanding as John. A New Testament and New Covenant apostle of the Lord Jesus Christ affirms that man can only baptize with water. Let us see the continuity of this message between John the Baptist and Matthew. Both the Old Testament prophet and the New Testament apostle have agreed on this matter that Jesus is the one who baptizes with the Holy Spirit (salvation) and fire (judgment).

Mark's Theology on Who Baptizes with the Holy Spirit

Mark 1:8—I baptize you with water, but he will baptize you with the Holy Spirit.

Mark, also known as John Mark, was a close companion of the apostle Peter and is also found many times in the Book of Acts. John Mark was a cousin of Barnabas (Colossians 4:10), who accompanied Paul and Barnabas on Paul's first missionary journey (Acts 12:25, 13:5). However, he deserted them along the way in Pamphylia and returned to Jerusalem (Acts 13:13). When Barnabas wanted Paul to take Mark on the second missionary journey, Paul refused. The friction that resulted between Paul and Barnabas led to their separation (Acts 15:38–40). However, even though Mark had left Barnabas and Paul in the first missionary journey, there was evidence that Mark had developed great strength and maturity and had proven himself to Paul. When Paul wrote to the Colossians, he instructed them that if John Mark came, they were to welcome him (Colossians 4:10). Paul also calls him a "fellow worker" in Philemon 24. Paul also writes to Timothy and tells him to get Mark and bring him because Mark was helpful to Paul in his ministry (2 Timothy 4:11). Lastly, Peter refers to Mark as "a son" in 1 Peter 5:13, "She who is in Babylon, chosen together with you, sends you her greetings, and so does my son Mark."

Mark, inspired by the Holy Spirit, has written down an abbreviated yet powerful statement on baptism with the Holy Spirit. He quotes John the Baptist where John says, "I baptize you with water, but he will baptize you with the Holy Spirit." Mark notes that John can only baptize with water, but the He, that is Christ, will baptize with the Holy Spirit. Mark also agrees that man can only baptize with water. Mark also agrees that only Christ can baptize with the Holy Spirit.

Let us pay attention to Mark's company. Mark was a useful worker to Paul. Mark was a spiritual son to Peter. Mark would have learned from both Peter and Paul. Mark would have known and agreed that man can only baptize with water, and Jesus was the only person who could baptize with the Holy Spirit. Peter and Paul would have agreed with this as well.

Luke's Theology on Who Baptizes with the Holy Spirit

Luke 3:16—John answered them all, "I baptize you with water. But one who is more powerful than I will come, the straps of whose sandals I am not worthy to untie. He will baptize you with the Holy Spirit and fire."

Luke was the Gentile author of the Gospel of Luke. Very little is known about Luke. He almost never included personal details about himself, and nothing definite is known about his background or his conversion. Luke was a frequent companion of the apostle Paul from the time of Paul's Macedonian vision (Acts 16:9–10) right up to the time of Paul's martyrdom (2 Timothy 4:11). The apostle Paul referred to Luke as "a doctor" (Colossians 4:14). Luke also penned the Book of Acts. Luke also dedicated his works to Theophilus as seen in Acts 1:1 and Luke 1:3. Luke also expressly states that his knowledge of the events recorded in his gospel came from the reports of those who were eyewitnesses (Luke 1:1–3). Luke also notes that his goal was to write an orderly account so that there would be certainty in the things Theophilus had been taught of Christ.

In Luke 3:16, Luke, who is inspired by the Holy Spirit, writes, "John answered them all, 'I baptize you with water. But one who is more powerful than I will come, the straps of whose sandals I am not worthy to untie. He will baptize you with the Holy Spirit and fire.'" Here, we note that Luke fully agrees with John the Baptist in that John can only baptize with water. John cannot baptize with the Holy Spirit. Likewise, men can only baptize with water. Men cannot baptize with the Holy Spirit. Only Christ can baptize with the Holy Spirit (salvation) and fire (judgment).

Let us note Luke's companions. Luke was a companion of the apostle Paul. Therefore, Luke would have been taught by Paul and would have had an agreement on water baptism and baptism of the Holy Spirit. Let us also note that Paul had a gospel. After Paul had been converted, he went to Arabia and then to

Damascus (Galatians 1:17–18). After three years, he went to Jerusalem and met with the leaders and those held in high esteem in Jerusalem (most likely the apostles) and presented them the gospel. The leaders noted that nothing needed to be added to Paul's message (Galatians 2:6). Let us also note that Paul would have had a clear understanding of water baptism and baptism with the Holy Spirit and who can baptize with the Holy Spirit. Luke, Paul, the apostles, and those held in high esteem would have agreed on this.

The Apostle John's Theology on Who Baptizes with the Holy Spirit

John 1:31–34—"I myself did not know him, but the reason I came baptizing with water was that he might be revealed to Israel." Then John gave this testimony: "I saw the Spirit come down from heaven as a dove and remain on him. And I myself did not know him, but the one who sent me to baptize with water told me, 'The man on whom you see the Spirit come down and remain is the one who will baptize with the Holy Spirit.' I have seen and I testify that this is God's Chosen One."

John was the younger brother of James, and both were known as "the sons of Zebedee." Jesus gave them the name "sons of thunder" (Mark 3:17). John was an apostle (Luke 6:12–16) and one of the three most intimate associates of Jesus along with Peter and James. John was an eyewitness to and participant in Jesus' earthly ministry (1 John 1:1–4). After Christ's ascension, John became a "pillar" in the Jerusalem church (Galatians 2:9). He ministered with Peter (Acts 3:1, 4:13, 8:14) and wrote the Book of Revelation (Revelation 1:1).

Here we have John the Apostle quoting from John the Baptist where John the Baptist says, "'The man on whom you see the Spirit come down and remain is the one who will baptize with the Holy Spirit.'" The apostle John, inspired by the Holy Spirit, would have agreed with John the Baptist. The apostle John would have agreed that man can only baptize with water. The apostle John would have agreed that man cannot baptize with the Holy Spirit. The apostle John would have agreed that only Christ can baptize with the Holy Spirit. Let us also note that John was one of the "pillars" in the early church. Let us also note that John was under Christ's teaching and would have known man's role in baptism and Christ's role in the baptism of the Holy Spirit. Let us see that John, inspired by the Holy Spirit, has drawn a distinction in roles between who baptizes with water and who baptizes with the Holy Spirit. Let's also note that John the Baptist says, "The man on whom you see the Spirit come down and remain is **the** one who will baptize with the Holy Spirit." John has used the definite article *the*. John does not use an indefinite article of *a*. No, John the Baptist is saying **"the" one** who will baptize with the Holy Spirit." This is none other than Jesus Christ. There is no other interpretation that can be made other than there is just one person who baptizes with the Holy Spirit while man can only baptize with water.

When looking at water baptism and baptism with the Holy Spirit, it is important to note what the Scriptures say about man's role in water baptism and Christ's role in baptism with the Holy Spirit. Matthew, Mark, Luke, the apostle John, and John the Baptist have clearly articulated their stance on who can baptize with the Holy Spirit and who can baptize with water. Let us note that man baptizes with water, but Christ baptizes with the Holy Spirit (salvation) and fire (judgment). Man's baptism cannot save. Christ baptizing with the Holy Spirit saves.

Chapter 4

Jesus' Theology on Water Baptism and Baptism with the Holy Spirit

Acts 1:4–5—On one occasion, while he was eating with them, he gave them this command: "Do not leave Jerusalem, but wait for the gift my Father promised, which you have heard me speak about. For John baptized with water, but in a few days you will be baptized with the Holy Spirit."

We would certainly want to pay attention to Jesus' thoughts on water baptism as well. Since all of Scripture is inspired by the Word of God, we can rest assured that there will and must be continuity on this matter of baptism with the Holy Spirit and baptizing with water. Therefore, let us examine Christ's words as He understands water baptism and baptism with the Holy Spirit.

Jesus had given His disciples or apostles the Great Commission which was to "go and make disciples of all nations, baptizing them in the name of the Father and of the Son and of the Holy Spirit, and teaching them to obey everything I have commanded you." Additionally, after His suffering, He presented Himself to the apostles and gave them many convincing proofs that He was alive. On one of these occasions with His disciples, Jesus talks about being baptized with the Holy Spirit. Luke writes in Acts 1:4–5, "On one occasion, while he was eating with them, he gave them this command: 'Do not leave Jerusalem, but wait for the gift my Father promised, which you have heard me speak about. For John baptized with water, but in a few days you will be baptized with the Holy Spirit.'" Shortly after He spoke this, He was taken up before the apostles and was seated at the right hand of His Father. Jesus promised on several occasions that He would send the promised Holy Spirit:

- Luke 11:13—If you then, though you are evil, know how to give good gifts to your children, how much more will your Father in heaven give the Holy Spirit to those who ask Him!
- Luke 24:49—I am going to send you what my Father has promised; but stay in the city until you have been clothed with power from on high.
- John 7:38-39—"Whoever believes in me, as Scripture has said, rivers of living water will flow from within them." By this he meant the Spirit, who those who believed in him were later to receive. Up to that time the Spirit had not been given, since Jesus had not yet been glorified.
- John 14:15–17—If you love me, keep my commands. And I will ask the Father, and he will give you another advocate to help you and be with you forever—The Spirit of truth. The world cannot accept him, because it neither sees him nor knows him. But you know him, for he lives with you and will be in you.
- John 14:26—But the Advocate, the Holy Spirit, whom the Father will send in my name, will teach you all things and will remind you of everything I have said to you.

- John 15:26—When the Advocate comes, whom I will send to you from the Father—the Spirit of truth who goes out from the Father—he will testify about me.
- John 16:7—But very truly I tell you, it is for your good that I am going away. Unless I go away, the Advocate will not come to you; but if I go, I will send him to you.

There are some very important points to understand about baptism with the Holy Spirit that must be pointed out in the verses that have been spoken by Jesus:

- The baptism of the Holy Spirit could not come until Jesus had ascended and been glorified. (John 7:39)
- Jesus would ask the Father for the Holy Spirit to be given. (John 14:16)
- The Holy Spirit would be given from the Father to the Son. (John 15:26; Luke 11:13 24:49)
- The Holy Spirit would be given from the Father in the Son's name. (John 14:26)
- Jesus would send the Holy Spirit. (John 16:7)
- The baptism of the Holy Spirit would be given to those who believe in Christ. (John 7:39)

Of course, it can be confusing to make sense of baptism of the Holy Spirit as Jesus describes it. One could ask the question whether the Holy Spirit comes from the Father or the Son. The answer would be both. The Spirit would proceed from the Father, the Son would ask for the Holy Spirit from His Father, and the Son would give the Holy Spirit. The intention is not to cause confusion around Jesus' explanation of baptism with the Holy Spirit, but it is important to note that Jesus did tell His apostles that John baptized with water but, in a few days, they would be baptized with the Holy Spirit which would proceed from Him. Let us note from Jesus that man cannot baptize with the Holy Spirit.

Let us also note that Jesus has drawn distinctions between water baptism and baptism with the Holy Spirit. Let us note according to Jesus that man can only baptize with water. Let us also note that the New Covenant includes man baptizing only with water, but Christ baptizing with the Holy Spirit. Let us remember Jesus' words to Nicodemus in John 3:6–8, "Flesh gives birth to flesh, but the Spirit gives birth to spirit. You should not be surprised at my saying, 'You must be born again.' The wind blows wherever it pleases. You hear its sound, but you cannot tell where it comes from or where it is going. So, it is with everyone born of the Spirit." Man cannot control the Holy Spirit through the rite or sacrament of water baptism. Man cannot control the Holy Spirit.

As we mentioned in chapter 3, a good understanding or definition of *baptism of the Holy Spirit* would be as follows: **The baptism with the Holy Spirit is the sovereign monergistic work of salvation performed by God the Father, God the Son, and God the Holy Spirit. The Holy Spirit is given from the Father to the Son and the Son pours out or gives the Holy Spirit in the Father's name. The Holy Spirit then regenerates or causes man to be born again through hearing the Word of God/Gospel which gives spiritual life to the previously spiritually dead man. God then grants man the ability to repent which is a gift and put saving faith in Jesus Christ which is also a gift. Man is then justified by grace through faith in Christ, receives and is indwelt by the Holy Spirit, and the Holy Spirit spiritually unites/immerses man with Jesus Christ and puts the man into the body of Christ. The baptism with the Holy Spirit is not water baptism and water baptism is not the baptism with the Holy Spirit for only Christ can baptize with the Holy Spirit and man can only baptize with water. The baptism with the Holy Spirit is a one-time, instantaneous, and salvific work of God.** This baptism with the Holy Spirit is, of course, a gift from God and not earned by man.

Not only did Christ affirm that John baptized with water and that He would baptize with the Holy Spirit (Acts 1:4–5), but He also gave His theology on whether water baptism was a work or not a work. In Matthew 3:13–15, we have an account of Jesus being baptized by John the Baptist:

Then Jesus came from Galilee to the Jordan to John, to be baptized by him. John would have prevented him, saying "I need to be baptized by you, and do you come to me?" But Jesus answered him, "Let it be so now, for thus it is fitting for us to fulfill all righteousness." Then he consented.

First, let's notice that John was startled by Jesus' request to be baptized. After all, John's baptism was for repentance and was offensive as we had learned earlier. Additionally, John had identified Jesus as being the Lamb of God who would take away the sins of the world (John 1:29). John would have felt totally inadequate to baptize Jesus for repentance when Jesus was the one who would baptize with the Holy Spirit and fire. Let's also notice that Jesus doesn't deny John's claim that he should be baptized by Jesus. Jesus also doesn't state that He needs the baptism for His own repentance as He has no sin.

Secondly, let's notice that Jesus said it is "fitting for us to fulfill all righteousness." What an interesting statement about Jesus needing to be baptized by John. In the original language, there are a couple words that stick out. The first word is translated "fitting" from the original word which is *prepon*. *Prepon* is a primitive verb meaning "tower up," "be conspicuous," or rather refers to acting appropriately in a particular situation (i.e., as it is seemly to God). The second word that stands out is translated "fulfill" from the original word which is *pléroó*. *Pléroó* means to "make full," "to complete," and, more properly, it means "to fill to individual capacity." The third word that stands out is *all* and from the original language which is *pas*. *Pas* means "all, the whole, every kind of" or, more properly, means "all" in the sense of each (every) part that applies. The last word that stands out is *righteousness* which in the original language is *dikaiosuné*. *Dikaiosuné* can also mean "the approval of God" and refers to "what is deemed right by the Lord." Putting this together we could also say Christ's statement this way:

- "It is seemly to God for us to fully complete all of God's divine standard."
- "It is right in the sight of God for us to fulfill all of righteousness required by God."

Jesus is, thus, calling baptism a work that is included in His perfect work. In 1 Corinthians 5:21, it says, "God made him who had no sin to be sin for us, so that in him we might become the righteousness of God." Part of Christ's righteousness included submitting to His Father's will to be baptized by John the Baptist. This is an important point that Christ is making. In some religious denominations, baptism is considered God working as the agent in baptism and, thus, is not a work. However, Christ categorizes water baptism as a work. Christ's water baptism was a part of His perfect, sinless life and righteousness that are given to men through faith in Jesus Christ. Therefore, calling water baptism anything but a work would be inaccurate according to Christ. It is good to remember that Christ fulfilled all righteousness on our behalf and that His perfect work is credited to our account through saving faith in Him. Water baptism cannot accomplish this.

Additionally, in Matthew 5:17, Jesus says, "Do not think that I have come to abolish the Law or the Prophets; I have not come to abolish them but to fulfill them." Jesus' sinless life, death, and resurrection are the imputed righteousness that He gives to those who come to Him in saving faith. Jesus fulfilled the prophecies. Jesus kept the law perfectly. Jesus fulfilled all righteousness on our behalf. Jesus identified baptism as a necessity to fulfill all righteousness so that we don't have to rely on baptism but on Christ alone through faith.

Scholars also note that Jesus identified with sinners and supported John the Baptist's ministry in his baptism of repentance. Both points are theologically sound. However, the point that is important in Jesus' teaching of water baptism and baptism with the Holy Spirit is that Jesus is the baptizer with the Holy Spirit and that water baptism is a work which man has been commanded to perform. Christ being baptized was considered a work to fulfill all righteousness. Jesus baptizes with the Holy Spirit and man can only baptize with water.

Lastly, we should take note of how water baptism should be thought of in terms of the baptism with the Holy Spirit. Water baptism serves as a sign of the New Covenant but also serves as a sign of the baptism with the Holy Spirit. In Matthew 28:19 Jesus says to His disciples, "Go therefore and make disciples of all nations, baptizing them in the name of the Father and of the Son and of the Holy Spirit". When thinking about the definition of the baptism with the Holy Spirit in light of Matthew 28:19, we can see how the Triune God is operating in salvation. With regard to water baptism, we can clearly see that water baptism symbolizes the baptism with the Holy Spirit. If we would refresh our memory of the definition of the baptism with the Holy Spirit we can see all that water baptism represents where: **the baptism with the Holy Spirit is the sovereign monergistic work of salvation performed by God the Father, God the Son, and God the Holy Spirit. The Holy Spirit is given from the Father to the Son and the Son pours out or gives the Holy Spirit in the Father's name. The Holy Spirit then regenerates or causes man to be born again through hearing the Word of God/Gospel which gives spiritual life to the previously spiritually dead man. God then grants man the ability to repent which is a gift and put saving faith in Jesus Christ which is also a gift. Man is then justified by grace through faith in Christ, receives and is indwelt**

by the Holy Spirit, and the Holy Spirit spiritually unites/immerses man with Jesus Christ and puts the man into the body of Christ. The baptism with the Holy Spirit is not water baptism and water baptism is not the baptism with the Holy Spirit for only Christ can baptize with the Holy Spirit and man can only baptize with water. The baptism with the Holy Spirit is a one-time, instantaneous, and salvific work of God.

Thus, when Jesus gives the command to baptize all nations in the name of the Father and of the Son and of the Holy Spirit, we can see that Jesus definitely had in mind that water baptism can and should be used to symbolize the baptism with the Holy Spirit and that the baptism with the Holy Spirit and water baptism are separate and distinct as water baptism serves as only a sign since man can only baptize with water while the baptism with the Holy Spirit is the sovereign monergistic work of salvation performed by the Triune God. Furthermore, we can see how both modes of baptism (sprinkling and immersion) capture different aspects of the baptism of the Holy Spirit. We can see this as the Holy Spirit is poured out on an individual (sprinkling/pouring) and we see the Holy Spirit immersing (immersion) and putting us into union with Christ. Thus, it would serve us well to impress upon our minds and hearts that a proper definition of the baptism with the Holy Spirit will give us a proper understanding of water baptism.

Chapter 5

Peter's Theology on Water Baptism and Baptism with the Holy Spirit

> *Acts 10:44–48—While Peter was still speaking these words, the Holy Spirit fell on all who heard the word. And the believers from among the circumcised who had come with Peter were amazed, because the gift of the Holy Spirit was poured out even on the Gentiles. For they were hearing them speaking in tongues and extolling God. Then Peter declared, "Can anyone withhold water for baptizing these people, who have received the Holy Spirit just as we have?" And he commanded them to be baptized in the name of Jesus Christ. Then they asked him to remain for some days.*

Acts 11:13–17—He told us how he had seen an angel appear in his house and say, "Send to Joppa for Simon who is called Peter. He will bring you a message through which you and all your household will be saved." As I began to speak, thc Holy Spirit came on them as he had come on us at the beginning. Then I remembered what the Lord had said: "John baptized with water, but you will be baptized with the Holy Spirit." So if God gave them the same gift he gave us who believed in the Lord Jesus Christ, who was I to think that I could stand in God's way?

Peter's "baptism now saves you" verse is one of the most quoted verses to support baptismal regeneration. We will get to that verse later, but it is important to note that Peter had the same understanding as Jesus when it came to water baptism and baptism with the Holy Spirit. In Acts 10, it becomes extremely clear that Peter was very aware that there was a difference between water baptism and baptism with the Holy Spirit and he was also aware of who baptizes with the Holy Spirit and who could only baptize with water. We will look to Acts 10 to reveal Peter's understanding of baptism with the Holy Spirit and water baptism.

Acts 10 is the account of the first Gentile conversion and Peter was privileged to experience this conversion. Acts 10 begins with Cornelius, a centurion in the Italian Regiment (Acts 10:1). Scripture explains that Cornelius was a Gentile and a devout and God-fearing man (Acts 10:2). Cornelius' faithfulness was seen as a memorial offering before God and he had received a vision and saw an angel of God who ordered him to send men to Joppa to bring Peter to his house (Acts 10:3–8).

The following day, Peter also had a vision where he saw heaven opened and something like a large sheet being lowered down to earth (Acts 10:9–11). It contained all kinds of animals, which included unclean animals as well as animals that conform to the Jewish dietary laws (Acts 10:12). This happened three times and Peter had wondered what the meaning of the vision meant (Acts 10:14–16). There are a couple of suggestions to what this vision may have meant. The first explanation is that this vision did away with the Jewish dietary laws. The voice told Peter to "Get up, Peter. Kill and eat." In Matthew 15:17–20, Jesus says, "Don't you see that whatever enters the mouth goes into the stomach and then out of the body? But the things that come out of a person's mouth come from the heart, and these defile them. For out of the heart come evil thoughts—murder, adultery, sexual immorality, theft, false testimony, slander. These are what defile a person; but eating with unwashed hands does not defile them." Additionally, in Mark 7:19, Mark concludes by saying, "For it doesn't go into their heart but into their stomach, and then out of the body." In saying this, Jesus declared all foods clean. In the original language it says, "Purifying all the food." The first interpretation is that in this vision, Jesus communicated the cessation of the dietary laws.

The second interpretation sees this vision as also having to do with Jews and Gentiles. In Leviticus 11, the LORD describes clean and unclean food. In this passage, there are reptiles such as the gecko, the crocodile, the sand reptile, and the chameleon. Likewise, the LORD also calls the eagle, the vulture, the buzzard, the red kite, the falcon, and more birds unclean. In Acts 10:15, the voice spoke to Peter saying, "Do not call anything impure that God has made clean." The interpretation sees the clean animals as the Jews and the unclean animals being the Gentiles. It is important to note that the sheet comes from heaven which signals that the church was born from heaven and includes both Jew and Gentile. Peter's vision was meant to communicate that the church, which came from heaven, was to include both the Jew and Gentile. After the vision, Cornelius' men found Peter at Simon the tanner's house (Acts 10:17–18). The men explained the vision that Cornelius had, and Peter invited them into his house (Acts 10:19–23).

The next day, Peter went with the men to Cornelius' house (Acts 10:24–26). When entering Cornelius' house, he interprets the vision where he says in verse 28, "But God has shown me that I should not call anyone impure or unclean." Peter communicates to the Gentiles in Cornelius' house that he is not to regard them as unclean anymore. Cornelius goes on to describe his vision to Peter (Acts 10:30–34). Peter then launches into a sermon on the gospel which includes peace through Jesus Christ who is Lord of all (Acts 10:36). Peter explains John the Baptist's baptism of repentance (Acts 10:37). Peter explains God anointing Jesus of Nazareth which would most certainly have included Him as the Son of God as well as the Christ (Acts 10:38). Peter explains Jesus' divine power over the devil and healing ministry (Acts 10:38). Peter explains Jesus' crucifixion (Acts 10:39). Peter explains Christ's resurrection (Acts 10:40). Peter explains Christ's post-resurrection appearances (Acts 10:41). Peter explains Christ as Lord and judge of all people (Acts 10:42–42). Finally, Peter explains Christ as the only means for forgiveness of sins (Acts 10:43).

Peter appeared to give a very good gospel presentation of Christ. Peter's gospel presentation included Christ as Lord of all and King of the kingdom of God (Acts 10:36), true repentance that bears fruit (Acts 10:37), Jesus' person as the Christ or Messiah (Acts 10:38), Jesus' work of divine power and authority (Acts 10:38), Jesus' work of salvation where He took the wrath of God to pay for the sins of His people (Acts 10:39), Christ's resurrection which confirmed Christ's work as sufficient to pay the debt for His people and victory over death, sin, and the devil (Acts 10:40), and the impending judgment and damnation for all those who would reject Christ as the means to forgiveness and eternal life (Acts 10:42–43). This was a very thorough presentation of the gospel.

While Peter had given the presentation of the gospel of Jesus, the Holy Spirit came on all who heard the message (Acts 10:44). Let us note that this is the baptism with the Holy Spirit. The Gentiles heard the good news of Jesus Christ, had believed, and thus received the promised Holy Spirit for believing in Christ (John 7:38–39). The Jews who were present were astonished that the Holy Spirit had been poured out to the Gentiles as was evidenced by the speaking in tongues (Acts 10:45–46). The same sign of speaking in tongues for the Jews on the day of Pentecost when they were baptized with the Holy Spirit was the same sign given to the Gentiles who believed and were baptized with the Holy Spirit.

Peter makes an amazing statement following the conversion of the Gentiles. Peter says in Acts 10:47–48, "'Can anyone withhold water for baptizing these people, who have received the Holy Spirit just as we have?' And he commanded them to be baptized in the name of Jesus Christ. Then they asked him to remain for some days." Peter has just made a distinction between baptism with the Holy Spirit and water baptism. Peter recognizes that *baptism with the Holy Spirit* includes when someone comes to faith in Jesus Christ and receives and is indwelt by the Holy Spirit. As Peter has recognized this, he commands them to be baptized in the name of Jesus Christ. Isn't this amazing? Just after the Gentiles had received the baptism with the Holy Spirit, Peter commands them to be baptized with water in the name of Jesus Christ. There is no doubt that Peter would have made strong and clear distinctions between who baptizes with the Holy Spirit and how man baptizes with water. We'll see this in Acts 11.

In Acts 11, the apostles and brothers throughout Judea heard that the Gentiles had received the word of God. The Jews, or the circumcision party, began to criticize Peter (Acts 11:1–3). However, Peter begins describing his vision to the men and then going to Cornelius' house (Acts 11:4–12). Picking up in Acts 11:14, Peter explains how Cornelius stated, "He will declare to you a message by which you will be saved, you and all your household." As we noted earlier, this was Peter's gospel presentation. In verses 15–16, Peter says, "As I began to speak, the Holy Spirit fell on them just as on us at the beginning. And I remembered the word of the Lord, how He said, 'John baptized with water, but you will be baptized with the Holy Spirit.'" Peter's theology in verses 15 and 16 cannot be understated. As Peter began to speak the gospel, the Gentiles were baptized with the Holy Spirit as they believed the gospel. Peter goes on to make an important point. Peter notes that Jesus said that John baptized with water but Peter would have also remembered John's words when John said, "But one who is more powerful than I will come, the straps of whose sandals I am not worthy to untie. He will baptize you with the Holy Spirit and fire." Peter would have known that man can only baptize with water and Christ is the one who baptized with the Holy Spirit. He heard this from Jesus and he heard this from John the Baptist. In fact, in verse 17, Peter says, "If then God gave the same gift to them as he gave to us when we believed in the Lord Jesus Christ, who was I that I could stand in God's way?" Furthermore, immediately after Peter realized the Gentiles had been baptized with the Holy Spirit, he ordered them to be water baptized. Peter had very clear theology on baptism with the Holy Spirit and water baptism and was able to distinguish between the two baptisms. Let us also remember that Peter was an apostle of Christ. Peter was witness to John's baptism and the Lord's teaching on baptism with the Holy Spirit. Let us remember that Peter quoted the Lord when saying, "'John baptized with water, but you will be baptized with the Holy Spirit.'" Man cannot baptize with the Holy Spirit and give life. Only Christ can baptize with the Holy Spirit.

Chapter 6

Paul's Theology on Water Baptism and Baptism with the Holy Spirit

1 Corinthians 12:13—For in one Spirit we were all baptized into one body, whether Jews or Greeks, whether slaves or free, and we were all made to drink of one Spirit.

Paul perhaps has some of the most difficult verses that he presents with regard to baptism. Indeed, he has verses in Romans 6:3–4 which say, "Or do you not know that all of us who have been baptized into Christ Jesus have been baptized into His death? Therefore, we have been buried with Him through baptism into death, so that, just as Christ was raised from the dead through the glory of the Father, so we too may walk in newness of life. Additionally, he has another difficult verse in Galatians 3:27 which says, "For all of you who were baptized into Christ have clothed yourselves with Christ. Some of these verses seem to indicate that Paul is at odds with Matthew, Mark, Luke, John, John the Baptist, Jesus, and Peter. However, Paul gives his theology of baptism with the Holy Spirit in

1 Corinthians 12. We will explain the Romans 6 and Galatians 3 verses later, but for now, let's focus on Paul's theology of baptism with the Holy Spirit.

In 1 Corinthians 12, Paul is addressing spiritual gifts to believers. As you read through the book of 1 Corinthians, you see quite a mess that Paul is dealing with in the Corinthian church. Paul has to straighten out division in the church (1 Corinthians 1:10–13), Paul had to deal with quarreling and jealousy amongst the believers (1 Corinthians 3:1–9), Paul had to clarify the need for servanthood (1 Corinthians 4:1–13), Paul had to deal with sexual immorality and incest in the church (1 Corinthians 5:1–13), Paul had to deal with believers bringing lawsuits against each other and bringing each other to court (1 Corinthians 6:1–8), Paul had to deal with sexual immorality in the church (1 Corinthians 6:12–20), Paul had to deal with marriage and sexual life (1 Corinthians 7:1–16), Paul had to deal with the use of Christian freedom (1 Corinthians 8–11:1), and Paul had to deal with the corruption that was taking place with the Lord's Supper (1 Corinthians 11:17–34). As we transition into chapter 12, we will see how Paul needs to explain the spiritual gifts to the Corinthians.

Paul begins explaining that there are different gifts given to believers and there is diversity in the body of Christ. However, the diversity is meant to build up the body of Christ for the common good. Paul's argument here is that although there are several different gifts that are distributed by one Spirit, all these different gifts are meant for the building up and nourishing of believers. He is emphasizing that although there is diversity, there must also be unity. If there is only diversity and no unity, the gifts are not being used properly (1 Corinthians 12:7, 11). Paul will go on to describe how all the gifts are analogous to the body in that a body is one but made up of many parts (1 Corinthians 12:14). He further goes on to explain that no body part should despise another body part as they accomplish their own task (1

Corinthians 12:15–23). Paul even explains that those body parts that are not as visible in the church may be seen as weaker but may be more honorable. Paul goes on explaining this unity in that Christ has put everything together and created the body so that there is no division and that all body parts should have equal concern for one another (1 Corinthians 12:25–26). Sandwiched between 1 Corinthians 12:1–12, where Paul talks about different gifts, and 1 Corinthians 12:14–26, where he talks about the body being diverse but in unity, Paul gives a very concise theology on baptism with the Holy Spirit in verse 13.

Paul says, starting in verse 13, "For in one Spirit we were all baptized into one body, whether Jews or Greeks, whether slaves or free, and we were all made to drink of one Spirit." Paul here is talking about Spirit baptism. The first point to note is that there is one Spirit that baptizes into one body. Jesus gives the explanation of baptism with the Holy Spirit in John 7:38–39 where He says, "Whoever believes in me, as the Scripture has said, 'Out of his heart will flow rivers of living water.'" Now, this he said about the Spirit, whom those who believed in him were to receive, for as yet the Spirit had not been given, because Jesus was not yet glorified." Jesus is explaining that when one has repented and come to saving faith in Him, he would receive the Holy Spirit. Another way of stating it is when anyone comes to saving faith in Jesus Christ, they are baptized with the Holy Spirit. The person who has come to saving faith in Christ receives the following and more:

- Justification and right standing with God (Romans 3:22–28)
- Adopted into the family of God (Ephesians 1:5)
- Declared a child of God (Romans 8:16)
- Given the Holy Spirit as a deposit (2 Corinthians 1:22)
- Forgiven of all sins (Hebrews 8:12)

- Raised up with Christ and seated in the heavenly realm (Ephesians 2:6)
- Coheirs with Christ (Romans 8:17)
- Receive Christ as our Great High Priest (Hebrews 4:14)
- Receive God as our Father (Romans 8:15)
- Receive Christ as our brother (Hebrews 2:11–12)
- Eternal life (John 17:3)

The same event took place with the first Gentile converts in Acts 10:44–45, when Peter gave a Gospel presentation and the Gentiles believed the message, "While Peter was still speaking these words, the Holy Spirit came on all who heard the message. The circumcised believers who had come with Peter were astonished that the gift of the Holy Spirit had been poured out even on Gentiles." Paul also makes a definitive statement about when one receives the Holy Spirit where he is confronting the Galatians who are giving ear to a false works-based gospel in Galatians 3:1-2 where he says, "O foolish Galatians! Who has bewitched you? It was before your eyes that Jesus Christ was publicly portrayed as crucified. Let me ask you only this: Did you receive the Spirit by works of the law or by hearing with faith?". Paul reiterates that the Holy Spirit is received through faith in Jesus Christ where Paul also says in Galatians 3:14, "He redeemed us in order that the blessing given to Abraham might come to the Gentiles through Christ Jesus, so that by faith we might receive the promise of the Spirit."

First, let's notice that *Baptism with the Holy Spirit* can be synonymous to coming to faith in Christ where the individual would receive the Holy Spirit and be put into the body of believers. Therefore, Paul's understanding of baptism with the Holy Spirit is that when one is baptized with the Holy Spirit, that person has put their faith in Jesus, receives the Holy Spirit, is put into the body of Christ, and placed into the kingdom of God. Let's all note that this is once again a gift from God and not a work.

Second, let's pay attention and note that he is talking in the past tense. Paul is stating that this occurred in the past and is not to be repeated. As noted in regeneration, just as there is one physical birth, for the believer, there is only one spiritual birth. No one is born from above multiple times. There is one spiritual birth that takes place which never happens again.

Third, we must ask who is the one who baptizes with the Holy Spirit. From our earlier points, we would note that it is Jesus Christ who baptizes with the Holy Spirit according to Matthew (3:11), Mark (1:8), Luke (3:16), the apostle John (1:33), John the Baptist (Matthew 3:11, Mark 1:8, Luke 3:16, John 1:33), Jesus (Acts 1:4–5), and Peter (Acts 11:16). This point has been emphasized earlier in more detail.

Fourth, let us note that baptism with the Holy Spirit was given regardless of social status. Paul describes that race was not a determining factor as it did not matter being a Jew or Gentile, or on job status when he describes slave or free. Paul may have had the prophet Joel's prophecy in mind where Joel said, "And in the last days it shall be, God declares, that I will pour out my Spirit on all flesh, and your sons and your daughters shall prophesy, and your young men shall see visions, and your old men shall dream dreams;" Joel was looking forward to the time when the Holy Spirit would be poured out on all flesh regardless of race, age, social status, and others.

Fifth, Paul's last theological point on baptism with the Holy Spirit is found in the following statement, "We were all made to drink of one Spirit." Once again, this highlights the sovereign saving work of God. God acts monergistically in regeneration. God gives the gift of repentance. God gives the gift of faith. God pours out the Holy Spirit. Paul's statement speaks to the sovereign saving work of God. This statement also hearkens back to the new covenant promise found in Ezekiel 36:26–27 where the LORD says, "I will give you a new heart and put a new spirit in you; I will remove from you your heart of stone and give you a heart of flesh. And I will put my Spirit in you and move you to follow my decrees and be careful to keep my laws." It is God who makes us to drink of His Spirit. It is God who puts His Spirit in us. Additionally, Paul could have had John 7:37 in mind, where Jesus said, "Let anyone who is thirsty come to me and drink. Whoever believes in me, as Scripture has said, rivers of living water will flow from within them." This also speaks to those who take this free gift of salvation and come to saving faith in Christ. God's gift is for the thirsty, the hungry, the destitute, the sick, the sinner, the poor in spirit, those mourning over sin, and those submitting to Christ in meekness. God puts His Spirit in anyone who comes to Him in saving faith and those who come to saving faith are the ones who are made to drink of the one Spirit. This statement speaks of God's sovereignty in salvation without denying man's will and responsibility to respond to Christ through faith.

Paul's Water Baptism Distinction

When Paul is confronting the Corinthians over their divisions, he also makes a powerful statement about water baptism. Starting in 1 Corinthians 1:13–17, Paul says, "Is Christ divided? Was Paul crucified for you? Were you baptized in the name of Paul? I thank God that I did not baptize any of you except Crispus and Gaius, so no one can say that you were baptized in my name. (Yes, I also baptized the household of Stephanas; beyond that, I don't remember if I baptized anyone else.) For Christ did not send me to baptize, but to preach the gospel—not with wisdom and eloquence, lest the cross of Christ be emptied of its power." In these passages, Paul makes a distinction in water baptism against preaching the gospel, which includes the priority and power of the gospel over water baptism.

First, Paul notes that the priority of preaching the gospel is far superior to water baptism. Paul does not downplay the importance of water baptism but does note that this was a much lower priority in the fact that he baptized only a few but preached the gospel to many. Paul only recalls baptizing two people and a household. In fact, the message of Christ crucified was the first priority (1 Corinthians 1:21–24; 15:1–4). Preaching Christ crucified was Paul's goal. In fact, in 1 Corinthians 9:16, Paul says, "Woe to me if I do not preach the gospel." Paul's priority was not water baptism but preaching the gospel. In fact in 1 Corinthians 1:17, he says, "For Christ did not send me to baptize, but to preach the gospel—not with wisdom and eloquence, lest the cross of Christ be emptied of its power." Paul is saying the gospel was the priority. The gospel of Christ is what saves, not water baptism.

Second, note the power of preaching the gospel over water baptism. In 1 Corinthians 1:18, Paul says, "For the message of the cross is foolishness to those who are perishing, but to us who are being saved it is the power of God." Paul's gospel message had the power to save. Paul never gave such power to water baptism. Paul actually thanked God that he didn't baptize many of the Corinthians. Here Paul is giving thanks for the lack of baptisms that he performed! Let us note where the power to save is. The gospel message is powerful to save as it describes man's condition and shows that faith in Christ is the only way to be saved. Salvation is not found in water baptism. Paul could make no such statement that baptism saves. However, Paul was able to say that the gospel message was powerful to save (1 Corinthians 1:18–31).

In summary, Paul was able to make a clear distinction between the priority and power of preaching the gospel over water baptism. Paul also had a theology of baptism with the Holy Spirit and water baptism that agreed with Matthew, Mark, Luke, the apostle John, John the Baptist, Peter, and Jesus.

CHAPTER 7

Paul's Theology on the Efficacy of Rituals and Sacraments on Salvation

Romans 4:9–12—Is this blessing then only for the circumcised, or also for the uncircumcised? For we say that faith was counted to Abraham as righteousness. How then was it counted to him? Was it before or after he had been circumcised? It was not after, but before he was circumcised. He received the sign of circumcision as a seal of the righteousness that he had by faith while he was still uncircumcised. The purpose was to make him the father of all who believe without being circumcised, so that righteousness would be counted to them as well, and to make him the father of the circumcised who are not merely circumcised but who also walk in the footsteps of the faith that our father Abraham had before he was circumcised.

Paul has organized Romans in such a way as to describe and outline the gospel. If we are to understand Paul's baptism verses in Romans 6, we must first understand his gospel presentation leading up to those verses. Additionally, prior to coming to chapter 4 of Romans, it is very beneficial to understand an overview of the first three chapters of Romans as we transition to Romans 4. A very good outline of Romans goes as such:

1. Introduction (1:1–17)
2. Justification by Faith (1:18–11:36)
   a. Sin—The "Need" for Salvation
      i. The Need of the Gentiles (1:18–2:16)
      ii. The Need of the Jews (2:17–3:8)
      iii. The Universal Need for Salvation (3:9–20)
   b. Justification by Faith—The "Provision" Made for Salvation
      i. God's Righteousness through Faith (3:21–31)
      ii. Abraham as an Example (4:1–25)
         1. **Justification Not through Works (4:1–8)**
         2. **Justification Not through Sacraments, Ceremonial Rites, or Rituals (4:9–12)**
         3. **Justification Not through the Law (4:13–25)**
   c. Freedom—The "Result" of Salvation
      i. Freedom from Wrath (5:1–21)
      ii. Freedom from Sin (6:1–23)
      iii. Freedom from the Law (7:1–25)
   d. Jew and Gentile—The "Scope" of Salvation
      i. God Chooses to Save Believers (9:1–33)
      ii. Israel Chose to Trust in Their Own Righteousness (10:1–21)
      iii. Both Jew and Gentile Can Have Salvation through Faith (11:1–36)
3. The Transformed Life (12:1–15:13)

   a. In Relation to Overall Conduct (12:1–21)
   b. In Relation to Civil Authority (13:1–7)
   c. In Relation to Fellow Man (13:8–14)
   d. In Relation to Weak Brethren (14:1–15:13)
4. Concluding Remarks, Instructions, and Benediction (15:14–16:27)

Paul has carefully outlined the book of Romans to highlight the result of our salvation which is that justification is by faith in Christ. Paul explains in Romans 1:18–3:20 that all men stand condemned under the wrath of God and that there is no one righteous in the sight of God. In Romans 3:21, Paul starts explaining and declaring the righteousness that comes by faith. Paul says that the righteousness is given through faith in Jesus Christ to all who believe (Romans 3:22), that all are justified freely by His grace through the redemption that came by Christ Jesus (Romans 3:24), that God presented Christ as the atonement for sin through the shedding of His blood which is received by faith (Romans 3:25), that God is just in punishment of sins but also the justifier to those who have faith in Jesus (Romans 3:26), that man is justified by faith and not by works (Romans 3:28), that God justifies the circumcised by faith and the uncircumcised through that same faith (Romans 3:30). Transitioning into Romans 4, Paul will explain how we are not justified.

Justified by Faith and Not Works

Paul's continued argument through the book of Romans continues to emphasize that man is justified by faith in Christ. In contrast, Paul will also describe how a man is not justified in Romans 4. Paul's argument is that Abraham would have understood that he was not justified by works, but by faith which God would then credit His perfect righteousness to Abraham (Romans 4:1–3). Paul also uses Scripture as his evidence that justification has always been by faith (Romans 4:3). Paul is stating that since the time of Abraham, man has always been justified by faith. Faith in God, but now more specifically, faith in Christ is how a man is justified and made right before God. In fact, the writer of Hebrews agrees with Paul on this same argument. In Hebrews 11:4–8, he says:

"By faith Abel brought God a better offering than Cain did. By faith he was commended as righteous, when God spoke well of his offerings. And by faith Abel still speaks, even though he is dead. By faith Enoch was taken from this life, so that he did not experience death: 'He could not be found, because God had taken him away.' For before he was taken, he was commended as one who pleased God. And without faith it is impossible to please God, because anyone who comes to him must believe that he exists and that he rewards those who earnestly seek him. By faith Noah, when warned about things not yet seen, in holy fear built an ark to save his family. By his faith he condemned the world and became heir of the righteousness that is in keeping with faith. By faith Abraham, when he called to go to a place he would later receive as his inheritance, obeyed and went, even though he did not know where he was going."

Paul is showing that faith had always been the instrument of salvation since Abraham until Christ comes again. The writer of Hebrews is saying that even dating back to the Fall in Genesis 3, faith saved even in the time of Adam. If Abel would have been saved through faith and since Adam and Eve were still alive as they had Seth after the death of Abel, then faith was the instrument of salvation even back to the time of Adam. Faith in God had always been the saving instrument of man, but in the last days and to be more specific, faith in Christ is what saves and justifies man.

The righteousness needed to stand before God without condemnation required a righteousness that man did not possess because man was found guilty before God (Romans 3:10–12).

Therefore, by faith, God's righteousness is credited to man. Paul goes on to further explain that if Abraham could not have worked for this righteousness because in Romans 4:1, he reasons those wages are not credited as a gift but as an obligation. Therefore, the logic follows that since it says that God credited righteousness to Abraham, then Abraham could not have earned this righteousness. If Abraham could work for his salvation, then God would have been obligated to give the righteousness to Abraham as a wage and not as a gift. However, in verse 5, Paul says that the one who does not work, but trusts God, this faith is credited as righteousness. Paul makes a closed case for dealing with a righteousness that can be worked for or earned in Romans 4:1–5. Paul uses Abraham as the example that no man can earn or work for his righteousness as all our righteous acts are as filthy rags (Isaiah 64:6).

In verses 6–8, he quotes Psalm 32, which comes from David after he had committed adultery with Bathsheba. David says, "Blessed is the one whose transgressions are forgiven, whose sins are covered. Blessed is the one whose sin the LORD does not count against them." Paul's point is that David knew the blessing of imputed righteousness. David knew that he could not stand before the LORD in his own righteousness. In fact, in Psalm 51:12, David says, "Restore to me the joy of your salvation and grant me a willing spirit, to sustain me." Notice that David didn't say, "Restore my salvation" or "Restore the righteousness you imputed," but says, "Restore to me the joy of your salvation." David is talking about the joy of knowing his salvation. Even more pointedly, David calls it, "your salvation." You can almost hear Paul sounding like David in Romans 11:36 where Paul says, "For from him and through him and to him are all things." David knows that his salvation is from the LORD and not by works. This is why Paul quotes David in Psalm 32. After such a serious sin, David's guilt is outweighing his joy of salvation. In verses 6–8, Paul is hearkening back to the great King David and quoting

David after he had known that his sins had been forgiven and he was still right before God based on his faith in the LORD.

Justified by Faith and Not Sacraments and Ceremonial Rites and Rituals

After Paul explains that justification does not take place based on man's works, he transitions over to ask whether the blessedness or righteousness that God gives is only for the circumcised or uncircumcised. Once again, he states that Abraham's faith was credited to him as righteousness, and he asks if this righteousness was credited to Abraham before or after he was circumcised. Paul concludes that the credited righteousness was given before and not after circumcision. Abraham was justified by faith before he was circumcised. In fact, Abraham was seventy-five when he was first called by God (Genesis 12), he was eighty-six when Ishmael was born (Genesis 15), and Abraham was ninety-nine when he was circumcised (Genesis 17). Paul goes on to explain that Abraham received circumcision as a sign, a seal of the righteousness, that he had by faith while he was still uncircumcised (Acts 4:11). Additionally, Paul says that he is the father of all who believe but have not been circumcised as well (Acts 4:11). Paul also adds that Abraham is the father of the circumcised who not only are circumcised but who follow in the footsteps of faith that Abraham had before he was circumcised (Acts 4:12).

Paul is aggressively arguing that circumcision does not save. Paul makes the same argument in Philippians 3:2-3 where he says, "Beware of the dogs, beware of the evil workers, beware of the false circumcision; for we are the true circumcision, who worship in the Spirit of God and take pride in Christ Jesus, and put no confidence in the flesh." In Philippians, Paul is arguing that no work, ritual, ceremony, has no merit as it relates to man being justified before God. Additionally, in Romans 2:28-29 Paul says, "For he is not a Jew who is one outwardly, nor is circumcision that which is outward in the flesh. But he is a Jew who is one inwardly; and circumcision is of the heart, by the Spirit, not by the letter; and his praise is not from people, but from God." In essence, Paul is stating in Romans 2:28-29, that the outward sign of faith which is circumcision, is not what saves, but rather the Spirit of God who performs heart surgery on man by removing the heart of stone and putting in a heart of flesh (Ezekiel 36:26). Paul is simply stating that the act of a ritual, ceremony, or sacrament is not what changes a man, but the Spirit of God. Likewise, Paul is making the argument that no outward sign of faith such as circumcision saves, but only serves as a sign and seal. Likewise, Paul is making an argument that water baptism will not save as it is only a sacrament or rite. Paul is stating that sacraments, rituals, and rites do not save. The Lord's Supper does not save. Baptism does not save. It can be argued that baptism has replaced circumcision as the new covenant sign of faith and serves as a sign and seal (Colossians 2:11–13). Baptism would serve as a sign to point to Christ. This sign of baptism would signify the regeneration of the Holy Spirit, the baptism with the Holy Spirit, being immersed in Christ's life, death, and resurrection, the washing away of sins, and more.

Baptism would serve as a seal; which is to say that if any man comes to Christ in faith, God guarantees with His seal that all the benefits included with faith in Christ will be given to believers. In ancient times, a king would use the signet on his ring to seal a letter with wax. The signet would be imprinted into the letter to show the authenticity of the letter and that it was from the king. The sign points towards Christ. Water baptism carries with it the seal of God which serves as an authentic promise for all those who come to saving faith in Christ that all the promises that baptism symbolizes will be given to them. All the promises of the New Covenant and promises which baptism represents are given to those who come to Christ in saving faith.

Paul not only makes the argument in Romans that outward ceremonial rituals and sacraments do not save, but he also does so in Galatians. Paul makes the same argument in Galatians chapters 2–3 where he states that no one is justified by works of the law. He states in Galatians 3:11, "Clearly no one who relies on the law is justified before God, because "the righteous will live by faith."

An even more astonishing remark he makes is in Galatians 5:3–4, "Again I declare to every man who lets himself be circumcised that he is obligated to obey the whole law. You who are trying to be justified by the law have been alienated from Christ; you have fallen away from grace." This is an incredible statement. Paul is stating that those who rely on works or sacraments and rituals are severed from Christ. The original language of being severed is *katargeo*, which means to "render inoperative, abolish." It is taken from two words which are *kata* and *argeo*. *Kata* is an intensifying word which strengthens *argeo*, which means "inactive or idle." Effectively, Paul is saying that you are completely done away with Christ and abolished if you try and trust in your works, circumcision, baptism, the Lord's Supper, or any other rite or ritual. Paul is saying that if you're hoping in Christ as well as your baptism, you're lost and you know not Christ! I believe Paul would even say that if you are trusting 99% in Christ and 1% in your baptism for your salvation, that you have been completely cut off from Christ. I even believe that Paul would say if you're trusting 99.9% in Christ and 0.01% in your baptism for salvation, that you are completely cut off from Christ. That is how severe Paul treats a *works salvation*, or salvation through sacraments and ceremonial rites. Paul says something similar in Galatians 6:15, where he says, "Neither circumcision nor uncircumcision means anything; what counts is the new creation." He is essentially saying the same thing as he has said about sacraments earlier. They have no power to save. Circumcision does not save. Baptism does not save. Works do not save. Faith in Christ is what saves. In

Galatians 5:3 and 6:15, Paul is warning that if anyone relies on sacraments, rituals, or ceremonies for their salvation, they are alienated from God and damned.

Let's remember Paul was a Pharisee prior to conversion and studied under the most prominent Pharisee, Gamaliel (Acts 22:3). Let's remember that Paul, who was a Pharisee prior to conversion, believed that one became ceremonially unclean by not washing one's hands before eating (Matthew 15:1-9). Let's remember that Paul would have been well educated in all the ceremonial washings that were required in the Old Testament which never brought the Israelites into the Most Holy Place. Let's remember, that Paul would know that none of the ceremonial washings, circumcision, offerings, and more never brought the people into the Most Holy Place or gave them right standing before God. Let's also remember that Paul puts no confidence in the flesh for salvation (Philippians 3:3), puts no confidence in ritualism/sacramentalism for salvation (Philippians 3:5), puts no confidence in national heritage for salvation (Philippians 3:5), puts no confidence in religious achievement for salvation (Philippians 3:5), and puts no confidence in law keeping ability for salvation (Philippians 3:7). In fact, Paul believed all those things are rubbish/skybala as it pertains to salvation as he says in Philippians 3:7-9, "But whatever gain I had, I counted as loss for the sake of Christ. Indeed, I count everything as loss because of the surpassing worth of knowing Christ Jesus my Lord. For his sake **I have suffered the loss of all things and count them as rubbish**, in order that I may gain Christ and be found in him, not having a righteousness of my own that comes from the law, but that which comes through faith in Christ, **the righteousness from God that depends on faith**". Let's also note that Paul drew distinctions between a spiritual circumcision (Romans 2:28-29, Colossians 2:11), and a circumcision with the flesh (Romans 2:28-29, Romans 4:9-12, Galatians 5:6, 6:15, 1 Corinthians 7:19).

Let's also note that Paul distinguished between a water baptism (1 Corinthians 1:17) and a Spirit baptism (1 Corinthians 12:13).

Justified by Faith and Not by Law Keeping

Paul has just cemented that justification does not come from works, sacraments, or ceremonial rites, and now he is going to emphasize that salvation does not come from keeping of the law in verses 13–25 of Romans 4. For the purposes of this book, I will not work to expound this text, but only mention it to help emphasize Paul's point that justification is not from works, which would include baptism according to Jesus, not from ceremonial rites or sacraments, and not from observance of the law.

In summary, Paul makes it abundantly clear how man is justified, which is by faith. A gospel which includes man being saved through works, sacraments, or ceremonial rites, or law observance is a false gospel. Such a gospel would greatly clash with Paul's understanding of justification by faith. Likewise, Paul would have strong objections towards water baptism having the efficacy to save as is indicated in Romans 4 and Galatians chapters 2, 3, 5, and 6.

Chapter 8

Understanding Peter's First Sermon on Pentecost and His Statement on Baptism

Acts 2:38 "Peter replied, 'Repent and be baptized, every one of you, in the name of Jesus Christ for the forgiveness of your sins. And you will receive the gift of the Holy Spirit.'"

We have established that Matthew, Mark, Luke, the apostle John, John the Baptist, Peter, Paul, and Jesus knew that man could only baptize with water and that only Christ could baptize with the Holy Spirit. In fact, in Acts 1:4–5, after Jesus had resurrected from the dead and shown himself to the apostles, He told them, "Do not leave Jerusalem, but wait for the gift my Father promised, which you have heard me speak about. For John baptized with water, but in a few days, you will be baptized with the Holy Spirit." *Pentecost* was the day that the Holy Spirit came and indwelt the believers, put them into the body of Christ, and filled them. It is important to note that the baptism with the Holy Spirit is different from being filled with the Holy Spirit, but, for the purposes of this book, we will not focus on the difference. However, a good short, definition of *being filled with the Holy Spirit* is as follows: **Being filled with the Holy Spirit is being submitted, affected, and influenced by the Holy Spirit to do His will.** Only believers can be filled with the Holy Spirit.

When the Holy Spirit came, God-fearing Jews heard the loud, violent blowing sound and then found that everyone along with the apostles were speaking in tongues or known languages and declaring the wonders of God. Those who heard this were amazed, astonished, and perplexed by what this meant. On the other hand, there were others that mocked the apostles and other believers, claiming that they were full of wine or drunk. This is where we'll pick up Peter's first sermon.

Acts 2:14–15—But Peter, standing with the eleven, lifted up his voice and addressed them: "Men of Judea and all who dwell in Jerusalem, let this be known to you, and give ear to my words. For these people are not drunk, as you suppose, since it is only the third hour of the day."

As Peter launches into his sermon to the Jerusalem audience, notice that Peter is taking his stand with the eleven apostles and, likewise, the eleven apostles are standing with Peter. Peter is about to take a stand for Christ and demands the attention of his audience. Notice that the crowd would most likely be hostile. Just fifty days prior to Pentecost, Christ had been put to death. Christ had been sentenced to crucifixion by a Jewish mistrial, undergone a Roman mistrial, and was betrayed by a Jewish population that had once cried hosanna to the Son of David. This same crowd ended up screaming for Christ's execution. Peter's audience could have included Pharisees and other Jewish leaders and it could have also included the Jewish crowds that pled for the execution of Christ. In any case, Peter, now filled with the Holy Spirit and who about fifty days earlier had been afraid of a servant girl, was now going to testify for Christ. Peter's testimony about Christ could have landed him with the same fate as Christ.

Announcing Jesus as the Christ could have drawn the same ire of the Pharisees. However, it didn't matter to Peter. Notice that he will give a testimony concerning Christ as the risen Messiah. Peter first rebukes the crowd and tells them that they aren't drunk as it's 9 a.m.

Acts 2:16–21—"And in the last days it shall be, God declares, that I will pour out my Spirit on all flesh, and your sons and your daughters shall prophesy, and your young men shall see visions, and your old men shall dream dreams; even on my male servants and female servants in those days I will pour out my Spirit, and they shall prophesy. And I will show wonders in the heavens above and signs on the earth below, blood, and fire, and vapor of smoke; the sun shall be turned to darkness and the moon to blood, before the day of the Lord comes, the great and magnificent day. And it shall come to pass that everyone who calls upon the name of the Lord shall be saved."

After Peter explains that the apostles and believers are not drunk, he explains what has happened. Peter explains that this is a prophecy that has been fulfilled by the prophet Joel. Joel's prophecy had indicated that the pouring out of the Spirit would occur before God would bring judgment on the world. The judgment day was and is known as the "Day of the LORD."

First, let's take notice that the people would have known what the day of the LORD would have looked like. This was portrayed as a day of darkness and gloom (Joel 2:2). This is a day of clouds and blackness (Joel 2:2). This is a day where an army of strength never seen would come (Joel 2:2). This is a day where fire devours and consumes everything in its way (Joel 2:3). This is a day the army's appearance is one of strength and causes nations to tremble (Joel 2:4–5). This is a day where the army destroys its opponents with ease (Joel 2:6–9). This is a day the earth shakes (Joel 2:10). This is a day the heavens tremble (Joel 2:10). This is a day the stars fail (Joel 2:10). This is a day the LORD is captain of the hosts (Joel 2:11). This is a day the LORD's armies cannot be counted (Joel 2:11). This is a day which is dreadful (Joel 2:11). They knew that the Day of the LORD was a day that would be filled with both deliverance and judgment. Additionally, in verse 32, it says, "And everyone who calls on the name of the LORD will be saved." This means that all those that do not call on the name of the LORD will be judged and those who call on the name of the LORD will be saved.

Second, the Jews would know that the Day of the LORD would not only be dreadful, but a day of judgment and deliverance. Not only would the Jews have known about the Day of the LORD, but they would also have believed that this prophecy would indicate that the Day of the LORD would be coming soon as the prophet Joel said this would happen in the "last days." Since the Spirit of the LORD had been poured out on all flesh, they would have known that they were in the last days. Also note that this Scripture that Peter quotes mentions "all who call upon the name of the LORD shall be saved." Peter will give a very firm answer on whose name to call on in verse 36, "Let all the house of Israel therefore know for certain that God has made him both Lord and Christ, this Jesus whom you crucified."

Third, the people would know that they were not in possession of the Holy Spirit. They saw the sign of tongues and believers glorifying the Lord and knew that the Spirit had not been poured out on them as they were not in possession of this same gift. According to the prophecy of Joel, they would be under divine judgment, and all the terror of the Day of the LORD would be theirs to experience in a judgment/non-deliverance way.

Fourth, they would have begun to understand baptism with the Holy Spirit. It was noted in the gospels that John the Baptist reiterated his statement about Messiah which can be found in Luke 3:16, "John answered them all, 'I baptize you with water. But one who is more powerful than I will come, the straps of whose sandals I am not worthy to untie. He will baptize you with the Holy Spirit and fire.'" Peter is going to explain that Jesus is the

Christ and Lord in verse 36. The people Peter is addressing could have made the connection that either the Spirit would be poured out on them by Christ (i.e., baptized with the Holy Spirit) or they would be baptized with fire and experience the Day of the LORD (i.e., judgment). They would have also realized that this outpouring of the Holy Spirit was not done by man.

Fifth, let's notice that the prophet Joel agreed with who was the baptizer in the baptism with the Holy Spirit. In Joel 2:28–29, notice that God says, "I will pour out my Spirit on all flesh" and "I will pour out my Spirit in those days and they will prophesy." Notice the "I" statement. It is God who pours out His Spirit. It is not man who pours out the Spirit. The Jews would have known that this outpouring of the Holy Spirit was not something that men did, but God. Joel's understanding of who baptizes with the Holy Spirit would have agreed with Matthew, Mark, Luke, the apostle John, John the Baptist, Peter, Paul, and Jesus.

Acts 2:22—Men of Israel, hear these words: Jesus of Nazareth, a man attested to you by God with mighty works and wonders and signs that God did through him in your midst, as you yourselves know.

After Peter explains the pouring out of the Holy Spirit which would indicate also being in "the last days" and the Day of the LORD was near, he moves to talk about the person and work of Jesus. Any complete presentation of the gospel will include the person and work of Jesus. Peter announces that Jesus of Nazareth was a man attested to the people by God with mighty works and wonders and signs that God did through Christ. The word *attested* is *apodeiknumi* in the original language. *Apodeiknumi* means to demonstrate, set forth, show by proof or properly demonstrating that something is what it "claims to be." Peter is saying that Jesus' messiahship should have been no surprise. You can almost hear Peter making the following points to the people about Jesus' demonstration of divine power, signs, and works:

- Did you not hear the voice from Heaven saying, "This is my Son, whom I love; with him I am well pleased." At Jesus' baptism? (Matthew 3:17)
- Did you not hear or see when Jesus turned water into wine? (John 2:1–11)
- Did you not hear or see when Jesus healed the royal official's son in Capernaum who was close to death? (John 4:43–54)
- Did you not hear or see when Jesus healed the man who was possessed by a demon? (Luke 4:31–37)
- Did you not hear or see when Jesus healed Peter's mother? (Luke 4:38–41)
- Did you not hear or see when Jesus healed the man with leprosy? (Luke 5:12–16)
- Did you not hear or see when men lowered the paralytic through the roof and Jesus healed him? (Luke 5:17–26)
- Did you not hear or see when Jesus healed the man who was invalid for thirty-eight years at the Bethesda pool? (John 5:1–47)
- Did you not hear or see when Jesus healed the man with the shriveled hand? (Matthew 12:9–14)
- Did you not hear or see how Jesus healed all of those from Judea, Jerusalem, and from the coastal region around Tyre and Sidon who came to hear Him and be healed of their diseases? (Luke 6:17–19)
- Did you not hear or see when Jesus healed the Centurion's servant? (Luke 7:1–10)
- Did you not hear or see when Jesus raised the widow's son from the dead? (Luke 7:11–17)
- Did you not hear or see when Jesus healed the demon possessed in Gadarenes and sent the demons into pigs? (Luke 8:26–39)
- Did you not hear or see when Jesus healed Jairus' daughter from the dead? (Luke 8:40–56)

- Did you not hear or see when Jesus healed two blind men? (Matthew 9:27–31)
- Did you not hear or see when Jesus healed the mute demon-possessed man? (Matthew 9:32–34)
- Did you not hear or see when Jesus fed five thousand? (Luke 9:10–17)
- Did you not hear or see when Jesus was in Gennesaret that all the people from that region carried the sick to Him and all who touched even the edge of His cloak were healed? (Mark 6:53–56)
- Did you not hear or see when Jesus healed the Syrophoenician woman's daughter from demon possession? (Mark 7:24–30)
- Did you not hear or see when Jesus went through Sidon, down to the Sea of Galilee and into the region of the Decapolis, that Jesus healed a deaf and mute man? (Mark 7:31–37)
- Did you not hear or see when Jesus fed the four thousand? (Mark 8:1–9)
- Did you not hear or see when Jesus healed the boy with the impure spirit? (Matthew 17:14–21)
- Did you not hear or see when Jesus healed the crippled woman on the Sabbath? (Mark 13:10–17)
- Did you not hear or see when Jesus healed the man born blind? (John 9:1–41)
- Did you not hear or see when Jesus healed the ten lepers? (Luke 17:12–19)
- Did you not hear or see when Jesus healed blind Bartimaeus? (Matthew 20:29–34)
- Did you not hear about the sky going black during the crucifixion of Christ? (Luke 23:44)
- Did you not feel the earth shake, see rocks split, and hear of the curtain leading into the Most Holy Place being torn when Christ died? (Matthew 27:51)

Peter is stating that there was more than enough evidence demonstrated which would lead the Jews to understand that Jesus was the Christ and sent by God. Even Jesus' teaching was amazing. In Matthew 7:28–29 it says, "When Jesus had finished saying these things, the crowds were amazed at his teaching because He taught as one who had authority, and not as their teachers of the law." Literally, the people were struck out of their senses and dumbfounded by Jesus' teaching as His teaching carried an authority that the people had never seen, a divine authority. Even the non-Jewish population knew there was something different about Jesus' teaching. In John 7:46, the temple guards said, "No one ever spoke the way this man does." Peter is saying to the Jewish audience this day that Jesus' teaching and His works were so divine and obvious that they should have believed Jesus' claims to deity and Messiah (John 8:58, Luke 4:17–30).

Acts 2:23–24—This Jesus, delivered up according to the definite plan and foreknowledge of God, you crucified and killed by the hands of lawless men. God raised him up, loosing the pangs of death, because it was not possible for him to be held by it.

Peter now talks about the sovereignty and omniscience of God the Father. Peter exclaims that Jesus was delivered up to death according to the sovereign plan of God. The Jews would be familiar with God's sovereignty, foreknowledge, and predestined plan. The story of Joseph would have crystalized this in their minds. Joseph, in Genesis 50:20, says, "As for you, you meant evil against me, but God meant it for good, to bring it about that many people should be kept alive, as they are today" and explains that he knew God was sovereign and at work when he was betrayed and left for dead by his brothers. However, Joseph's imprisonment and trials ultimately led to his rise in Egypt to serve the Pharaoh. All of this was a part of God's divine plan. Likewise, back in eternity past, God the Father knew of this plan that the Jews would kill Jesus. Christ's death didn't happen by accident. God the Father didn't look into the future and see that His Son would be betrayed and then try to find a way to deal with it. No, God the Father is omniscient and, when Christ was served up to be crucified for the sins of His people, everything was going exactly to the Father's plan.

Isaiah 53 speaks to this very clearly which was a seven-hundred-year-old prophecy about the crucifixion of Christ. Psalm 22, which was written about by David, was about a thousand-year-old prophecy which was also a prophecy of the crucifixion of Christ. In fact, crucifixion had not yet been invented when Psalm 22 was written. This is how exact and definite the plan of God was and is. Also, notice that although this was the sovereign plan of God in eternity past, Peter lays the blame on the Jewish crowd. He says, "You crucified and killed by the hands of lawless men." Although the sovereign plan of God was to have Jesus killed and crucified, this did not neglect human responsibility. The crowd as well as the Sadducees and Pharisees, along with Pontius Pilate and the Jewish crowd, all had blood on their hands. Peter is saying, "You are the ones who killed God's Son. Pilate and the religious teachers may have sentenced and gave Him a mistrial, but you are still the ones who murdered Him when you screamed, 'Crucify him. Crucify him.'"

Although Jesus was crucified, Peter explains that God raised Him from the dead. Peter will go on to explain what this means by quoting Psalm 16.

Acts 2:25–28—For David says concerning him, "'I saw the Lord always before me, for he is at my right hand that I may not be shaken; therefore my heart was glad, and my tongue rejoiced; my flesh also will dwell in hope. For you will not abandon my soul to Hades, or let your Holy One see corruption. You have made known to me the paths of life; you will make me full of gladness with your presence."

Peter goes on to quote David from Psalm 16. However, as we learn from Peter, Psalm 16:8–11 is written by David, but the one speaking in these verses is Jesus Christ. When you read the "I," "me," and "my" in this section, this is really Jesus speaking.

When Jesus says, "I saw the Lord always before me, for he is at my right hand that I may not be shaken; therefore my heart was glad, and my tongue rejoiced; my flesh also will dwell in hope," this is a prophecy where Jesus is speaking with confidence that He always sees His Father and is always doing His will. This can be spoken of throughout Jesus' life as He lived in total submission to His Father (John 5:19), even as Jesus headed to Gethsemane to be handed over to the Jewish leaders and ultimately be crucified. This speaks to Jesus' confidence in the Father's plan. Jesus saw the task ahead and said, "Not my will but your will be done" (Luke 22:42). Jesus knew the crown of thorns, the mocking, the beating, the flogging, the crucifixion, and more were all awaiting Him but what troubled His heart to the point of death was facing the wrath of God for the sins of His people (Mark 14:34). However, Jesus still always saw the Lord before Him and was not shaken. Jesus did not do His will but fulfilled His Father's will and was not shaken from completing His work.

Jesus goes on to say, "For you will not abandon my soul to Hades, or let your Holy One see corruption. You have made known to me the paths of life; you will make me full of gladness with your presence." This speaks to Jesus' unwavering belief in His Father glorifying Him and His work. If the Son had failed in His mission to live a perfect and sinless life, the Son would stay in the ground and be counted as a sinner. However, since the Son's work was perfect and sinless, Jesus was sure that His Father would glorify Him and raise Him from the dead. This ultimately speaks to the resurrection. No gospel presentation is complete without the resurrection. The resurrection speaks to Christ's victory over sin, death, and the devil. Jesus was not a victim at Calvary, He was a victor. Jesus was not defeated at Calvary, but dominant. Upon the cross, Jesus did not say "I am finished," but "It is finished." Peter did not exclude the resurrection which speaks to the Father's approval of Christ's work by raising Him from the dead, but speaks to the perfect completion of Christ's work.

Acts 2:29–33—"Brothers, I may say to you with confidence about the patriarch David that he both died and was buried, and his tomb is with us to this day. Being therefore a prophet, and knowing that God has sworn with an oath to him that he would set one of his descendants on his throne, he foresaw and spoke about the resurrection of the Christ, that he was not abandoned to Hades, nor did his flesh see corruption. This Jesus God raised up, and of that we all are witnesses. Being therefore exalted at the right hand of God, and having received from the Father the promise of the Holy Spirit, he has poured out this that you yourselves are seeing and hearing."

First, Peter further exposits Psalm 16 and explains that David had died, was buried, but had not been resurrected. However, David was a prophet and knew that God swore an oath to him that his house, throne, and kingdom would last forever (2 Samuel 7:8–16, 27–29). Peter is explaining that God's oath to David has been fulfilled and that the descendant from David, Christ, had established a kingdom that would reign forever as Jesus had not only been resurrected, but also ascended.

Second, another point of Peter's gospel presentation included the ascension of Christ. A complete gospel presentation will also include the ascension. This speaks of Christ's earthly work being complete. There is no more earthly ministry for Christ. He has completed everything needed for the salvation of men. Christ is seated at the right hand of God the Father, which means that Jesus has equal status to the Father and has been fully glorified.

Third, Peter talks about Christ receiving the promised Holy Spirit from the Father and has poured out the Spirit which is what the people were seeing and hearing. It's important to think back of what Jesus had promised to His disciples. Jesus had told them that He was going to go away and send the promised Holy

Spirit (John 16:7). Jesus also said that those who believed in Him would receive the promised Holy Spirit (John 7:38–39). Here, Peter once again explains that Jesus is the one who baptizes with the Holy Spirit. Jesus' work was complete and had received the Holy Spirit from the Father which He was able to pour out. Once again, Matthew, Mark, Luke, the apostle John, John the Baptist, the prophet Joel, Jesus, Paul, and Peter all had the same understanding of who baptizes with the Holy Spirit and pours out the Holy Spirit, Christ.

- Luke 24:49—I am going to send you what my Father has promised; but stay in the city until you have been clothed with power from on high.
- John 7:38–39—"Whoever believes in me, as Scripture has said, rivers of living water will flow from within them." By this he meant the Spirit, who those who believed in him were later to receive. Up to that time the Spirit had not been given, since Jesus had not yet been glorified.
- John 14:15–17—If you love me, keep my commands. And I will ask the Father, and he will give you another advocate to help you and be with you forever—The Spirit of truth. The world cannot accept him, because it neither sees him nor knows him. But you know him, for he lives with you and will be in you.
- John 14:26—But the Advocate, the Holy Spirit, whom the Father will send in my name, will teach you all things and will remind you of everything I have said to you.
- John 15:26—When the Advocate comes, whom I will send to you from the Father—the Spirit of truth who goes out from the Father—he will testify about me.
- John 16:7—But very truly I tell you, it is for your good that I am going away. Unless I go away, the Advocate will not come to you; but if I go, I will send him to you.

- Acts 2:34–36—For David did not ascend into the heavens, but he himself says, "'The Lord said to my Lord, 'Sit at my right hand, until I make your enemies your footstool."' Let all the house of Israel therefore know for certain that God has made him both Lord and Christ, this Jesus whom you crucified.

Peter notes that David never ascended into heaven but knew that the LORD would give all authority to someone. That someone, Peter is claiming, is Jesus Christ. In the original Hebrew language, it could also be translated, "YAHWEH said to my Adonai." This was a messianic passage of Scripture where it was prophesied by David that YAHWEH would give authority and power to David's Lord. In verse 36, Peter solves the mystery of who the Lord is. He says in verse 36, "Let all the house of Israel therefore know for certain that God has made him both Lord and Christ, this Jesus whom you crucified." What a statement! In Acts 2:21, Peter says that all who call on the name of the LORD will be saved and, in Acts 2:36, he says that the name that must be called on to be saved is Jesus. Peter has just called Jesus both the Messiah and Lord! Let's stop and pause to see what Peter has told the Jewish audience with regard to the gospel:

- That they were in the last days as the Spirit was being poured out on all flesh (Acts 2:17)
- That the prophecy of Joel spoke of the Day of the Lord which included divine judgment, wrath, and deliverance (Acts 2:19–21, Joel 2:28–32)
- Jesus' person and work being consistent with the Messiah (Acts 2:22–23)
- God's foreknowledge, sovereign, predetermined plan of Christ's crucifixion (Acts 2:23)
- Man's sin and guilt of crucifying the Messiah (Acts 2:23)

- God the Father raising Christ from the dead (Acts 2:24, 27, 31)
- Jesus being the ascended Messiah (Acts 2:32–33)
- Jesus' glorification as the Messiah (Acts 2:33)
- Christ as the baptizer with the Holy Spirit (Acts 2:33)
- Jesus as the Christ and Lord overall, equal with the Father (Acts 2:34–35)
- The Jewish audience as murderers and enemies of the Lord Jesus Christ (Acts 2:36)

Peter has just laid out an excellent gospel presentation. Peter has proven that Jesus is the Messiah as attested by the Father and evidenced by His Son's person and work. Peter has proven that Jesus is the resurrected Messiah. Peter has proven that Jesus is the ascended Messiah. Peter has proven that Jesus is the Lord. Peter has proven that Jesus is the Christ that the prophets had spoken of. Peter has spoken of God's plan of salvation. Peter has spoken of man's guilt and sin. Peter has spoken of Jesus as sovereign. Peter has spoken of Jesus as an enemy to those who have not accepted Him as Lord and Christ.

Acts 2:37—Now when they heard this they were cut to the heart, and said to Peter and the rest of the apostles, "Brothers, what shall we do?"

The Jewish audience was stunned. Peter had proved through Scripture that Jesus was the Christ, that they were in the last days, that the Spirit was poured out and they were not a part of the group of believers who had received the Holy Spirit, that Jesus was equal in power and status to God by being seated at the right hand of God, and that the enemies of the Lord Jesus were going to be Christ's footstool. The people could have also harkened back to John the Baptist's warning of Jesus being the Lord and Christ and His winnowing fork is in His hand separating the wheat from the chaff and the chaff being burned with unquenchable fire. The people could have also remembered John the Baptist warning of Jesus having an ax in His hand and the ax being at the root of the tree ready to chop down the tree and throw it in the fire. If the Jewish audience had followed along, they knew they were in trouble of divine judgment.

When it says the people were cut to the heart, this denotes a very strong reaction by the crowd. It's as if the veil had been taken away and they saw the atrocity that they had committed against God's Messiah. In fact, they interrupted Peter's sermon to ask what they must do. Peter was not yet done giving his speech when the people interrupted Peter's message and basically asked how they can be made right with God. They couldn't take another word from Peter, and they needed to stop Him and ask what the terms of peace were that God required. They saw themselves as enemies of God. They understood the footstool analogy which pictured God's foot on their necks and being moments away from delivering the final crushing blow to them. No wonder they cried out in the middle of his sermon to ask for the terms of peace with God.

Acts 2:38—And Peter said to them, "Repent and be baptized every one of you in the name of Jesus Christ for the forgiveness of your sins, and you will receive the gift of the Holy Spirit."

Peter's charge to them was that they killed the Messiah and were enemies with Jesus Christ and YAHWEH. Peter tells them to repent and be baptized. Some would point to this passage and say that baptism gives the forgiveness of sins, but this is not what Peter is saying. Peter is saying that since the Jews killed Jesus the Messiah, they must perform a complete 180 degree turn. Peter is saying that since they rejected Jesus as Lord and Christ, they must now surrender and trust Jesus as their Lord and Christ. Peter is telling them to abandon Judaism for Christ. Peter is telling them to stop following the Pharisees and Sadducees. Peter is telling them to be completely identified and surrendered to Jesus. The Jews would know that identifying with Jesus would potentially mean accepting the same fate the religious community and leaders gave to Jesus. This is no small repentance. This is a complete abandonment of the Jewish system. This is surrender to Jesus as the Lord and Messiah. This is willingness to pay the price for being associated with Jesus.

In Deuteronomy 13:6–15, it says:

> "If your brother, the son of your mother, your son or your daughter, the wife of your bosom, or your friend who is as your own soul, secretly entices you, saying, 'Let us go and serve other gods,' which you have not known, neither you nor your fathers, of the gods of the people which are all around you, near to you or far off from you, from one end of the earth to the other end of the earth, you shall not consent to him or listen to him, nor shall your eye pity him, nor shall you spare him or conceal him; but you shall surely kill him; your hand shall be first against him to put him to death, and afterward the hand of all the people. And you shall stone him with stones until he dies, because he sought to entice you away from the LORD your God, who brought you out of the land of Egypt, from the house of bondage. So all Israel shall hear and fear, and not again do such wickedness as this among you. If you hear someone in one of your cities, which the LORD your God gives you to dwell in, saying, 'Corrupt men have gone out from among you and enticed the inhabitants of their city, saying, "Let us go and serve other gods"'—which you have not known—then you shall inquire, search out, and ask diligently. And if it is indeed true and certain that such an abomination was committed among you, you shall surely strike the inhabitants of that city with the edge of

> the sword, utterly destroying it, all that is in it and its livestock—with the edge of the sword."

There was a cost in Judaism for going and serving other gods. Since the Pharisees, Sadducees, and religious leaders of that day did not see Jesus as the Christ or believe Jesus' claim to deity, they surely saw Him as a false god even after the resurrection. Anyone that would follow Jesus Christ would be subject to the same treatment as Jesus, crucifixion or perhaps stoning. It's also important to remember that many of the Jews saw Jesus as a heretic as claiming to be equal with God, claiming to be the Son of God, and claiming to be "I AM" (John 8:58), which was a claim to be YAHWEH.

Peter tells them to be baptized in the name of Jesus Christ for the forgiveness of sins. There are many sacramentalists who look to this passage and say that baptism is what gives forgiveness of sins, but Peter is not claiming that the baptism is what gives forgiveness. In fact, Peter understood John baptized with water, but Jesus would baptize with the Holy Spirit. Peter is calling for a public declaration and commitment to Christ as evidenced by being baptized in the name of Jesus Christ. Dr. Ryrie has said of baptism, "Even today for a Jew it is not his profession of Christianity nor his attendance at Christian services nor his acceptance of the New Testament, but today even, his submission to water baptism that definitely and finally excludes him from the Jewish community and marks him off as a Christian."

Since Peter has just proven that Jesus is the Messiah and the Jewish people are guilty of killing Him, he is commanding them to be public disciples and followers of Christ. He is calling them to abandon Judaism, to count their sacrifices as nothing, to count their circumcision as nothing, to count their righteous acts as nothing, and to trust in Christ completely and totally for salvation as evidenced by a public baptism in the name of Jesus Christ. This was an extreme repentance and call to the Jewish community.

You can clearly see Peter's understanding of Christ's evangelistic call to faith. This was a radical repentance. This was submission to Christ the King. Since Jesus was Lord over the kingdom of God or kingdom of heaven, there were certainly terms of surrender to enter Christ's kingdom. The kingdom has a king, and Christ would very often give His terms of surrender to enter this kingdom. You can see Peter's evangelistic call to become a disciple of Christ. You can also see that Peter evangelistically called people to repentance and saving faith or discipleship just as Jesus did.

- Matthew 10:37–39—Whoever loves father or mother more than me is not worthy of me and whoever loves son our daughter more than me is not worthy of me. And whoever does not take his cross and follow me is not worthy of me. Whoever finds his life will lose it, and whoever loses his life for my sake will find it.
- Matthew 16:24–26—Then Jesus told his disciples: "If anyone would come after me, let him deny himself and take up his cross and follow me. For whoever would save his life will lose it, but whoever loses his life for my sake will find it. For what will it profit a man if he gains the whole world and forfeits his soul? Or what shall a man give in return for his soul?"
- Mark 8:34–35—And calling the crowd to him with his disciples, he said to them: "If anyone would come after me let him deny himself and take up his cross and follow me. For whoever would save his life will lose it, but whoever loses his life for my sake and the gospel will save it. For what does it profit a man to gain the whole world and forfeit his soul? For what can a man give in return for his soul? For whoever is ashamed of me and of my words in this adulterous and sinful generation, of him will the Son of Man also be ashamed when he comes in the glory of his Father with the holy angels."

- Luke 9:23–26—And he said to all, “If anyone would come after me, let him deny himself and take up his cross daily and follow me. For whoever would save his life will lose it, but whoever loses his life for my sake will save it. For what does it profit a man if he gains the whole world and loses or forfeits himself? For whoever is ashamed of me and of my words, of him will the Son of Man be ashamed when he comes in his glory and the glory of the Father and of the holy angels.”
- Luke 14:25–33—Now great crowds accompanied him and he turned and said to them, “If anyone comes to me and does not hate his own father and mother and wife and children and brothers and sisters, yes and even his own life, he cannot be my disciple. Whoever does not bear his own cross and come after me cannot be my disciple. For which of you desiring to build a tower, does not first sit down and count the cost, whether he has enough to complete it? Otherwise, when he has laid a foundation and is not able to finish, all who see it begin to mock him saying, ‘This man began to build and was not able to finish.’ Or what king going out to encounter another king in war, will not sit down first and deliberate whether he is able with ten thousand to meet him who comes against him with twenty thousand? And if not, while the other is yet far off, he sends a delegation and asks for terms of peace. So therefore, any one of you who does not renounce all that he has cannot be my disciple.”
- John 12:24–26—Truly, truly, I say to you unless a grain of wheat falls into the earth and dies, it remains alone, but if it dies, it bears much fruit. Whoever loves his life loses it, and whoever hates his life in this world will keep it for eternal life. If anyone serves me, he must follow me, and where I am, there will my servant be also. If anyone serves me, the Father will honor him.

The Jewish audience would need to so identify with Jesus that they would deny themselves, take up their cross, and follow Him. This is what Peter was really commanding them to do. The people knew it and knew the consequences of such a decision. Peter is calling the Jews to Christ exactly how Jesus called people. Peter is telling them to count the costs and decide whether they will publicly declare Jesus as Lord and Christ even if it costs them their family and relationships, their personal ambitions, their personal sins, and their personal belongings. Peter is telling them to come all the way and publicly declare Jesus as Lord and Christ and to see Him as the only way to be made right with God and to completely surrender and trust in Jesus. This is what Peter was speaking of when he said, "Repent and be baptized every one of you in the name of Jesus Christ for the forgiveness of your sins, and you will receive the gift of the Holy Spirit."

Let's also note that those who would make such a commitment would receive the Holy Spirit. Let's note that although they were willing to give up everything they had and were, they would receive a gift much more precious than all creation. Those that surrender to Christ shall never be disappointed. Let's also note that all those that will give their life for Christ and the gospel must count the cost. It is costly to follow Jesus, but it is more costly not to follow Him.

Let's notice that it was not water baptism that saved. It was the response and gift of faith which surrenders to Christ and trusts Him alone for salvation that saves. This was a costly decision for the people as it meant giving up Judaism, losing family ties and relationships, losing status, and denying yourself as you've claimed Jesus as Lord of your life. Peter was faithful in his call to bring people to Christ. His evangelistic sermon included the full gospel which included the person and work of Christ, but also the response of faith. The first apostolic sermon should be an example of how we call people to faith in Christ. It is a tragedy to take this verse out of context and state that water baptism gives forgiveness of sins as this would completely ignore Peter's call to faith in Christ and put the emphasis on the sacrament giving salvation which was not Peter's intention.

Finally, in Acts 2:41, it says, "Those who accepted his message were baptized, and about three thousand were added to their number that day." It's important to note the extraordinary number of people converted through the preaching of the gospel. Surely, anyone would be overjoyed with 3,000 people choosing to follow and trust Christ. This should speak to the primacy of preaching the gospel by heralding it and proclaiming it, with great conviction and persuasion. Finally, let's also note how many people denied or had chosen not to be identified with Jesus. The Jewish historian Josephus made this observation about the attendance at the Passover feast during the days of Nero:

"So these high priests, upon the coming of their feast which is called the Passover, when they slay their sacrifices, from the ninth hour to the eleventh, but so that a company not less than ten belong to every sacrifice, (for it is not lawful for them to feast singly by themselves,) and many of us are twenty in a company, found the number of sacrifices was two hundred fifty-six thousand five hundred; which, upon the allowance of no more than ten that feast together, amounts to two million seven hundred thousand two hundred persons that were pure and holy."

The Passover was the main feast of the Jews, so it's very possible that the number was far less than two million seven hundred thousand. However, there were still men in Jerusalem this day from different parts of the world that were still in Jerusalem (Acts 2:8-11), so let's notice that even if there were one million people in Jerusalem and only three thousand identified and followed Christ, this would be 0.3% of the population. Regardless of the outcome, never stop preaching the gospel that Christ commanded men to preach. Never back down from proclaiming the extreme call to following Christ as found in Matthew 10:37–39, 16:24–26; Mark 8:34–35; Luke 9:23–26, 14:25–33; and, John

12:24–26. Whether you receive three thousand people that will follow Christ or if you will receive 3,000 stones as Stephen did, never be ashamed of the gospel of Christ.

Chapter 9

Understanding Paul's "Baptism" Verse in Romans 6

Romans 6:3–4—Do you not know that all of us who have been baptized into Christ Jesus were baptized into his death? We were buried therefore with him by baptism in death, in order that, just as Christ was raised from the dead by the glory of the Father, we too might walk in newness of life.

This is often cited as a definite defense that water baptism saves. In fact, if the Bible was given and only contained this verse, it would be definitive evidence to show that baptism does save. However, this is simply not the case. We must contend with the earlier points that were made regarding regeneration, water baptism, baptism with the Holy Spirit, and Paul's understanding of man being justified by faith and not by works, circumcision (including baptism), and observance of the law. To take this verse and understand that water baptism saves would pose the following problems:

- Jesus' teaching of regeneration or being born from above (John 3:3)

- Jesus' teaching of being born of water and the Spirit (John 3:5, Ezekiel 36:24–27)
- Nicodemus would not have understood being born of water and the Spirit as Christian baptism as this had not yet been instituted and Jesus was not talking about performing another ritual or sacramental ordinance to enter the kingdom of God. (John 3:5)
- Jesus' teaching on total depravity and flesh only producing flesh and sin (John 3:6)
- Jesus' teaching on the work of the Holy Spirit as being analogous to the wind, which is not controlled, coerced, or commanded (John 3:8)
- Jesus' teaching of the new birth, which is monergistic (John 3:1–10)
- The baptism of repentance for the forgiveness of sins as preached by John the Baptist was a radical call to repentance and not just another ritual. (Luke 3:3–16)
- The baptism of repentance didn't call for just being dipped in, sprinkled with, or immersed in water, but for a heart-searching repentance that elevated sin, brought down pride and self-righteousness, called for acknowledgement that Jews were no better than Gentiles, and called for a complete turning away of one's life in preparation for the Messiah. (Luke 3:3–16)
- Matthew understood that John and all other men could only baptize with water, but Christ could baptize with the Holy Spirit. (Matthew 3:11–12)
- Mark understood that John and all other men could only baptize with water, but Christ could baptize with the Holy Spirit. (Mark 1:8)
- Luke understood that John and all other men could only baptize with water, but Christ could baptize with the Holy Spirit. (Luke 3:16)

- The apostle John understood that John and all other men could only baptize with water, but Christ could baptize with the Holy Spirit. (John 1:31–33)
- John the Baptist understood that he and all other men could only baptize with water, but Christ could baptize with the Holy Spirit. (Matthew 3:11–12, Mark 1:8, Luke 3:16, John 1:31–33)
- Peter understood that he and all other men could only baptize with water, but Christ could baptize with the Holy Spirit. (Acts 2:17–18, 10:44–48, 11:16)
- Jesus understood that only He could baptize with the Holy Spirit and that men could only baptize with water. (Matthew 3:11–12; Mark 1:8; Luke 3:16, 24:49; John 1:31–33, 7:38–39, 14:15–17, 14:26, 15:26, 16:7; Acts 1:4–5, 2:17–18, 10:44–48, 11:16)
- Jesus understood baptism as a work and not baptism as God working through the baptism. (Matthew 3:13–15)
- Paul's understanding of baptism with the Holy Spirit (1 Corinthians 12:13)
- Paul's understanding of the power and position of water baptism in contrast with preaching the gospel (1 Corinthians 1:14–30)
- Paul's understanding of sacraments or signs and seals of faith, which include baptism, and that they had no power to justify man (Romans 4:1–17)

There is a mountain of concern with stating that water baptism saves as given by the evidence above which has been reviewed in previous chapters. If Romans 6:3–5 is to be taken as water baptism saving, this passage must deal with the points that have been mentioned above. To understand Romans 6:1–6 and get an understanding of this baptism verse, it would be good to refresh what Paul has laid out thus far in Romans. This outline is helpful to understand what Paul has said thus far regarding condemnation and justification. The following verses found in the respective sections of the outline will also help provide greater clarity:

1. Justification by Faith (Romans 1:18–11:36)
    a. Sin—The "Need" for Salvation
        i. Righteousness That Comes by Faith (Romans 1:16–17)
        ii. The Need of the Gentiles (Romans 1:18–2:16)
            1. Universal Condemnation of Man According to the Law
                a. Romans 2:1–5—Therefore you have no excuse, O man, every one of you who judges. For in passing judgment on another you condemn yourself, because you, the judge, practice the very same things. We know that the judgment of God rightly falls on those who practice such things. Do you suppose, O man—you who judge those who practice such things and yet do them yourself—that you will escape the judgment of God? Or do you presume on the riches of his kindness and forbearance and patience, not knowing that God's kindness is meant to lead you to repentance? But because of your hard and impenitent heart you are storing up wrath for yourself on the day of wrath when God's righteous judgment will be revealed.
        ii. The Need of the Jews (Romans 2:17–3:8)
            3. Romans 2:25–29—For circumcision indeed is of value if you obey the law, but if you break the law, your circumcision becomes uncircumcision. So, if a man who is uncircumcised keeps the precepts of the law, will not his uncircumcision be regarded as circumcision? Then he who is physically

uncircumcised but keeps the law will condemn you who have the written code and circumcision but break the law. For no one is a Jew who is merely one outwardly, nor is circumcision outward and physical. But a Jew is one inwardly, and circumcision is a matter of the heart, by the Spirit, not by the letter. His praise is not from man.

iv. The Universal Need for Salvation (Romans 3:9–20)

5. Romans 3:10–12—As it is written: "None is righteous, no, not one; no one understands; no one seeks for God. All have turned aside; together they have become worthless; no one does good, not even one."
6. Romans 3:18—"There is no fear of God before their eyes."
7. Romans 3:21—For by works of the law no flesh will be justified in his sight, since through the law comes knowledge of sin.

b. Justification by Faith—The "Provision" Made for Salvation

i. God's Righteousness through faith (Romans 3:21–31)

2. Romans 3:22–26—The righteousness of God through faith in Jesus Christ for all who believe. For there is no distinction: for all have sinned and fall short of the glory of God, and are justified by His grace as a gift, through the redemption that is in Christ Jesus, whom God put forward as a propitiation by His blood, to be received by faith. This was to show God's righteousness, because in His divine forbearance He had passed over former sins. It was to show his righteousness at the present time, so that he might be just and the justifier of the one who has faith in Jesus.

3. Romans 3:27–28—Then what becomes of our boasting? It is excluded. By what kind of law? By a law of works? No, but by the law of faith. For we hold that one is justified by faith apart from works of the law.

iv. Abraham as an Example (Romans 4:1–25)

1. Justification Not through Works (Romans 4:1–8)
   a. Romans 4:4–5—Now to the one who works, his wages are not counted as a gift but as his due. And to the one who does not work but believes in him who justifies the ungodly, his faith is counted as righteousness.
2. Justification Not through Sacraments, Ceremonial Rites, or Rituals (Romans 4:9–12)
   a. Romans 4:9–10—Is this blessing then only for the circumcised, or also for the uncircumcised? For we say that faith was counted to Abraham as righteousness. How then was it counted to him? Was it before or after he had been circumcised? It was not after, but before he was circumcised.
3. Justification Not through the Law (Romans 4:13–25)
   a. Romans 4:13–15—For the promise to Abraham and his offspring that he would be heir of the world did not come through the law but through the righteousness of faith. For if it is the adherents of the law who are to be the heirs, faith is null and the promise is void. For the law brings wrath, but where there is no law there is no transgression.

c. Freedom—The "Result" of Salvation

i. Freedom from Wrath (Romans 5:1–21)

1. Romans 5:1–2—Therefore, since we have been justified by faith, we have peace with God through our Lord Jesus Christ. Through him we have also obtained access by faith into this grace in which we stand, and we rejoice in hope of the glory of God.
2. Romans 5:17–21—For if, because of one man's trespass, death reigned through that one man, much more will those who receive the abundance of grace and the free gift of righteousness reign in life through the one man Jesus Christ. Therefore, as one trespass led to condemnation for all men, so one act of righteousness leads to justification and life for all men. For as by the one man's disobedience the many were made sinners, so by the one man's obedience the many will be made righteous. Now the law came in to increase the trespass, but where sin increased, grace abounded all the more, so that, as sin reigned in death, grace also might reign through the righteousness leading to eternal life through Jesus Christ our Lord.

This rough outline gives a very good overview of the first five chapters of Romans which clarifies that all men are condemned according to the law. He outlines that the condemnation is universal regardless of being Jew or Gentile. He outlines the condemnation is universal regardless of circumcision. He outlines that all men are condemned with no exception. He outlines that man is not justified by works.

The most troublesome point to deal with is that when approaching this verse, Paul has already declared that man is not saved by rituals or ceremonies. He outlines that man is not justified by circumcision or any other ritual or sacrament, which would include baptism. He outlines that justification comes through faith in Jesus Christ. This is what leads into Romans 6. The golden thread that runs through Romans 1–5 is justification by faith and condemnation for those whose hope of salvation is based on works, ceremonies, rites, rituals, and law observance.

Romans 6:1–2—What shall we say then? Are we to continue in sin that grace may abound? By no means! How can we who died to sin still live in it?

Paul, like any good teacher, has already anticipated his opponent's next question which is if we are justified by faith in Christ, won't this give a license to sin? Paul asks if we are saved by grace alone through faith alone in Christ alone, should we continue to sin as we are covered by grace? Paul declares, "*Mé genoito,*" which could be translated as follows:

- May this never come to pass.
- May this never happen.
- One thousand times "NO!"

He goes on to say, "How could someone who has died to sin still live in it?" This speaks to one doctrine that we have already discussed which is the Doctrine of Regeneration. Paul is arguing that if God has regenerated you or if you have been born from above, how could you possibly live in sin as if nothing happened? Paul is asking, "How could you have your heart of stone removed, be given a heart of flesh, be given a new spirit, and have the Holy Spirit put in you and continue to live in sin as a pattern of your life?" Paul is asking, "How is it possible that you are claiming union with Christ but continue in your sin as if nothing happened? How does the power of the Holy Spirit live in you and you desire to sin as you did before? How is it possible to have your nature completely changed with a new heart and new spirit and the Spirit of God within you and God's regenerative work makes no difference in your life regarding an unbroken pattern of sin?" Paul is making an argument that if you continue in sin so that grace may abound, this does not appear to be the regenerating work of God where He monergistically causes someone to be born from above.

As we'll see later, he is going to ask, "How is it possible to have union with Christ through faith and not be so changed in your inner person and with the power of the Holy Spirit?" Paul will argue that this is impossible. If God the Holy Spirit has regenerated you and changed you and the Holy Spirit lives in you, your relationship to sin will have changed. The sin you loved, you will reject. The Lord who had no control over your life is now your personal Lord and the master of your life through faith.

Here is an analogous story of what Paul is saying:

There was a pastor who was invited to a conference. The pastor showed up late and was asked to explain why he was not able to make it there on time. The pastor said that his Toyota Prius was in a head on collision with a semitruck that was carrying an excavator on the interstate at 70 miles per hour. The pastors all looked at each other and said, "That story makes no sense. How could you hit a semitruck carrying an excavator in your Toyota Prius at 70 miles per hour head on and be fine as if nothing happened to you? I mean look at you, you have no injuries, lacerations, or broken bones, and your car looks perfectly fine."

Paul's argument is the very same thing. he is saying, "How could you have encountered the Living God, had your nature changed by the regenerating power of the Holy Spirit, have union with Christ, have the Holy Spirit living in you, and not have a new relationship with sin?" Paul would say this is impossible. If you have union with Christ through faith, there will be a new relationship with sin. Although sin will still be present in your life, it is not your master (Romans 6:14). How could a new creature in Christ (2 Corinthians 5:17) continue living in sin as though nothing happened? Even worse, how could a new creature in Christ increase their sinfulness? Yes, there is still sin, but as Paul will explain in verses 3–6, there is a new master that you obey and there will be a new course and direction in your life because of the union with Christ. He'll go on in verses 15–22 and explain that you're either a slave to sin or a slave to Christ. There is no in between. You are either a slave to righteousness or a slave to sin.

Romans 6:3–Do you now know that all of us who have been baptized into Christ Jesus were baptized into his death?

Here is the verse that can often be pointed to and highlighted as the verse which declares that water baptism unites us with Christ. In fact, many Bible-believing scholars have interpreted this passage as water baptism bringing about unity with Christ. However, it is important to remember the passages and Scripture that have been explained in previous chapters. There are two explanations. Either this verse is speaking of water baptism or this is speaking of baptism with the Holy Spirit. Jesus, the apostles, and many others were able to draw distinctions between water baptism and baptism with the Holy Spirit and this verse demands this level of attention. Paul would undoubtedly be speaking of baptism with the Holy Spirit. For if water baptism could save, he would have baptized as many people as he could (1 Corinthians 1:14–30). However, Paul reasoned that preaching the gospel took priority because it had the power to save. He gave no such priority and power to water baptism. Additionally, he understood baptism with the Holy Spirit to include the operation where man was made to drink of the Spirit and be put into the body of Christ (1 Corinthians 12:13). It's also important to remember the definition of *baptism with the Holy Spirit*: **The baptism with the Holy Spirit is the sovereign monergistic work of salvation performed by God the Father, God the Son, and God the Holy Spirit. The Holy Spirit is given from the Father to the Son and the Son pours out or gives the Holy Spirit in the Father's name. The Holy Spirit then regenerates or causes man to be born again through hearing the Word of God/Gospel which gives spiritual life to the previously spiritually dead man. God then grants man the ability to repent which is a gift and put**

saving faith in Jesus Christ which is also a gift. Man is then justified by grace through faith in Christ, receives and is indwelt by the Holy Spirit, and the Holy Spirit spiritually unites/immerses man with Jesus Christ and puts the man into the body of Christ. The baptism with the Holy Spirit is not water baptism and water baptism is not the baptism with the Holy Spirit for only Christ can baptize with the Holy Spirit and man can only baptize with water. The baptism with the Holy Spirit is a one-time, instantaneous, and salvific work of God.

Lastly, we should see that Paul's argument has been that we are justified by faith in Christ throughout the whole book of Romans. He even stresses not being saved by works (Romans 4:1–8), not being saved through rituals or sacraments (Romans 4:9–12), and not being saved through observance of the law (Romans 4:13–24). To claim this passage as being water baptism is a serious misinterpretation of Scripture that does not square away or line up with Romans. In fact, interpreting this passage as water baptism giving union with Christ contradicts many other passages of Scripture, but would completely demolish the argument he made in Romans 4. Additionally, if water baptism justifies man, this would abruptly and awkwardly introduce a new means to be justified. Water baptism is the wrong interpretation. There are three verses that will help understand Romans 6:3-4 being a Spirit baptism versus a water baptism. These three verses are Romans 3:22, Galatians 3:2, and Ephesians 1:13. A helpful way of thinking about this Spirit baptism or baptism with the Holy Spirit according to Paul is that when one puts their faith in Christ (Romans 3:22), they receive the Holy Spirit (Galatians 3:2, Ephesians 1:13), and are put into the body of Christ and are united with Christ (1 Corinthians 12:13).

The question is: What is Paul saying here in verse 3? The word *baptized* can also mean "dip, submerged, or dip under." Baptism with the Holy Spirit would be the best explanation of this verse as Paul describes in 1 Corinthians 12:13, "For we were all baptized by one Spirit so as to form one body—whether Jews or Gentiles, slave or free—and we were all given the one Spirit to drink." Paul talks about the work of the Spirit putting us or immersing us into the body of Christ and, thus, giving us union with Christ. This union with Christ comes through faith in Christ. Paul's point is that through this spiritual baptism, we were immersed into Christ's death. In other words, the union that we have with Christ extends all the way back two thousand years ago. Because of our union with Christ through faith, we have been so immersed into Christ that we are identified into all His person and work. This is Paul's argument. If you have union with Christ, you have all the imputed work and righteousness that Christ attained, which includes His death.

Furthermore, Paul's explanation of the believer being immersed into Christ's death also emphasizes Christ crucified for sin. Christ the Savior had to go to the cross to pay the penalty for the sins of His people. Paul would have understood Isaiah's prophecy in Isaiah 53:

- Surely, he took up our pain and bore our suffering, yet we considered him punished by God, stricken by him, and afflicted. (v. 4)
- But he was pierced for our transgressions, he was crushed for our iniquities; the punishment that brought us peace was on him, and by his wounds we are healed (v. 5)
- We all like sheep, have gone astray, each of us has turned to our own way; and the LORD has laid on him the iniquity of us all. (v. 6)
- He was oppressed and afflicted, yet he did not open his mouth; he was led like a lamb to the slaughter, and as a sheep before its shearers is silent, so he did not open his mouth. (v. 7)
- By oppression and judgment he was taken away. Yet who of his generation protested? For he was cut off from the

land of the living; for the transgression of my people he was punished. (v. 8)

- Yet it was the LORD's will to crush him and cause him to suffer and though the LORD makes his life an offering for sin, he will see his offspring and prolong his days, and the will of the LORD will prosper his hand (v. 10)

Christ's once for all atonement for the sins of His people needed to be paid. Jesus took the wrath of God upon the cross (Isaiah 53:10). The only people who will know what Christ suffered on the cross are those who have rejected Him and are in hell. Christ paid that fine for us on the cross (Colossians 2:14). Christ took the sins of His people to the cross and defeated them, disarmed them, and made a spectacle of them (Colossians 2:15). For our sake, God made Him to be sin who knew no sin, so that in Him we might become the righteousness of God (2 Corinthians 5:21). Paul looks to the greatest sin in human history of putting Christ to death on the cross and then the greatest victory of Christ dying on the cross and says that those who have been united with Christ through faith have been immersed in Christ's death on the cross. The work that we could not do was done for us. In fact, the death He died, He died to sin once for all; but the life He lives, He lives to God (Romans 6:10). Peter says the same thing in 1 Peter 3:18, "For Christ also suffered once for sins, the righteous for the unrighteous, to bring you to God. He was put to death in the body but made alive in the Spirit." The writer of Hebrews says the same thing in Hebrews 9:26, "Otherwise Christ would have had to suffer many times since the creation of the world. But he has appeared once for all at the culmination of the ages to do away with sin by the sacrifice of himself."

Those united to Christ through faith were baptized with the Holy Spirit and have been immersed into Christ's death which did away with sins for His people. This is Paul's point in verse 3. This baptism with the Holy Spirit that is performed by Christ immerses us into union with Christ through faith and immerses us into Christ's death where our manner or walk of life is death to sin, but alive to God (Romans 6:10). This is Paul's point when he states we have been baptized into Christ. It is to say that our old life of sin is dead and our new manner of life is toward God's will.

Romans 6:4—We were therefore buried with him through baptism into death in order that, just as Christ was raised from the dead through the glory of the Father, we too may live a new life. For if we have been united with him in a death like his, we will certainly also be united with him in a resurrection like his. For we know that our old self was crucified with him so that the body ruled by sin might be done away with, that we should no longer be slaves to sin.

Once again, some may interpret this as water baptism, but, as noted above, this does not square away with Paul's flow of justification by faith in Romans and contradicts man baptizing with water versus Christ baptizing with the Holy Spirit. This verse would best be interpreted as buried with Him through Spirit baptism or, rather, baptism with the Holy Spirit.

Paul goes a step further. He not only says we were immersed into Christ's death, but we were also buried with Him through our union with Him, which comes by faith. Not only do we partake in Christ's death, but we participate in Christ's burial and His resurrection. Paul is saying that in our union with Christ, which comes by faith, we have all the blessing of having Christ's perfect work in life, Christ's perfect work on the cross, Christ's death, Christ's burial, Christ's resurrection, and, eventually, Christ's glorification. Note that this is also past tense. This happened because of our faith in Christ and was a one-time event. Paul is saying that when we were justified by the gift of faith in Christ, we went back two thousand years and were completely immersed in Christ's work. It's as if we were there on the cross with Christ and, just as Christ was raised from the dead, we too live a new life.

It's also important to note the statement "*Hēmeis en kainotēti zōēs peripatēsōmen.*" This is translated "We in newness of life should walk." The word *kainotés* means "freshness, newness, novelty." The lexicon explains this newness to produce a new state which is eternal life and can also mean, as in Romans 7:6, a new condition or state of (moral) life. The other word of note is *peripatēsōmen. Peripatēsōmen* means "I walk," hence, Hebraistically (in an ethical sense): I conduct my life, live. In other words, since we have been united to Christ in faith, there is a newness or novelty in how we live or walk. As we learned in Ezekiel 36:25–27, this new walk stems from a new heart, a new spirit, and God's Spirit within us. In fact, we were once dead in transgressions and sins and were children of wrath (Ephesians 2:1–3). However, because of God regenerating us and causing us to be born from above, we were also given the gift of faith in Christ which gives us union with Christ. And just as Christ was raised from the dead, we too live a new life. Paul also notes that there was an old self and that there was a time when this old self was a slave to sin (v. 6).

Paul goes on in verses 5–6 to talk about the implications of being united to Christ in His death and that there is certainty of transformation of life.

Therefore, Paul's argument from Romans 6:1–6 is that those who argue that the doctrine of justification by faith will create a license to sin are in serious error. Paul argues that the faith that justifies will bring about union and immersion into Christ's life. Therefore, we will be under the dominion and rule of the Lord rather than the dominion and rule of sin. Furthermore, there will be a transformation or, rather, regeneration of our lives. It will not be the old man with a new haircut or cosmetic surgery. No, this new man will have new affections, new desires, and a new direction of life because they have been regenerated, given a new heart, given a new spirit, and have the Spirit of Jesus Christ in them. How could such a person who is in union with Christ through faith go on sinning so that grace may increase? Paul's response: Impossible!

As you can see, Paul's argument was around the sanctification and walk of life of a person who had been justified by faith in Christ. Paul was not arguing for baptismal regeneration or that water baptism unites man to Christ. Such a reading of Romans 6:1–6 would negate Romans 1–5 and strike a serious blow against his argument for justification by faith in Christ.

CHAPTER 10

Understanding Paul's "Baptism" Verse in Galatians 3

Galatians 3:27—For as many of you as were baptized into Christ have put on Christ.

Another baptism verse comes from Paul's letter to the Galatians. Paul wrote Galatians to counter Judaizing false teachers who were undermining the central New Testament doctrine of justification by faith. They spread their dangerous teaching which taught that Gentiles must first become Jewish proselytes and submit to all Mosaic laws before they could become Christians. Shocked by the Galatians' openness to that damning heresy, Paul wrote this letter to defend justification by faith and warn these churches of the dire consequences of abandoning that essential doctrine. Galatians is the only epistle Paul wrote that does not contain a commendation for its readers—that obvious omission reflects how urgently he felt about confronting the defection and defending the essential doctrine of justification.

The central theme of Galatians is justification by faith. Paul defends that doctrine, which is the heart of the gospel, both in its theological and practical ramifications. He also defends his position as an apostle since, as in Corinth, false teachers had attempted to gain a hearing for their heretical teaching by undermining Paul's credibility. Galatians has been referred to as a mini-Romans as it contains many of the same theological themes such as the inability of the law to justify (2:16), the believer's deadness to the law (2:19), the believer's crucifixion with Christ (2:20), Abraham's justification by faith (3:6), that believers are Abraham's spiritual children (3:7) and therefore blessed, that the law brings God's wrath and not salvation (3:10), that the just shall live by faith (3:11), the universality of sin (3:22), that believers are spiritually baptized into Christ (3:27), believer's adoption as God's spiritual children (4:5–7), that love fulfills the law (5:14), the importance of walking in the Spirit (5:16), the warfare of the flesh against the Spirit (5:17), and the importance of believers bearing one another's burdens (6:2). Below is an outline of Paul's epistle to the Galatians:

1. Personal: The Preacher of Justification (1:1–2:21)
   a. Apostolic Chastening (1:1–9)
   b. Apostolic Credentials (1:10–2:10)
   c. Apostolic Confidence (2:11–21)
2. Doctrinal: The Principles of Justification (3:1–4:31)
   a. The Experience of the Galatians (3:1–5)
   b. The Blessing of Abraham (3:6–9)
   c. The Curse of the Law (3:10–14)
   d. The Promise of the Covenant (3:15–18)
   e. The Purpose of the Law (3:19–29)
   f. The Sonship of Believers (4:1–7)
   g. The Futility of Ritualism (4:8–20)
   h. The Illustration from Scripture (4:21–31)
3. Practical: The Privileges of Justification (5:1–6:18)
   a. Freedom from Ritual (5:1–6)
   b. Freedom from Legalists (5:7–12)
   c. Freedom in the Spirit (5:13–26)

d. Freedom from Spiritual Bondage (6:1–10)
e. Conclusion (6:11–18)

It's important to get an overview of Paul's epistle to the Galatians as this helps make sense of the doctrine of justification by faith, but also brings a stinging rebuke to anyone who would teach anything that would contradict this. Let's start in chapter 1.

As mentioned above, Galatians is the only epistle Paul wrote that does not contain a commendation for its readers—that obvious omission reflects how urgently he felt about confronting the defection from the true gospel and defending the essential doctrine of justification. He was quickly addressing the different gospel that was being taught and that was throwing people into confusion and was corrupting the gospel of Christ (v. 6–7). Paul's next statement should sink down in everyone's soul who would seek to be a teacher or preacher of the gospel. Paul says of those who would preach another gospel in verses 8–9, "But even if we or an angel from heaven should preach a gospel other than the one we preached to you, let them be accursed!" As we have already said, so now I say again: "If anybody is preaching to you a gospel other than what you accepted, let them be under God's curse!" This is a remarkable statement. Paul is saying that no matter who you are, if you preach a gospel other than the gospel of Christ, let whoever is doing that be accursed. The word *accursed* is translated from the original word *anathema,* which refers to God devoting someone to destruction in eternal hell. Notice that Paul says this twice in verses 8 and 9. Paul is saying it twice for extra emphasis on the danger of preaching another gospel. Paul's statement on preaching another gospel could be said this way as well:

- If you preach any gospel other than the gospel of Jesus Christ, God damn you to hell.

- If you preach a different gospel than Christ's gospel, let you be damned to hell.
- If you preach a gospel that perverts the person of Christ, the work of Christ, or justification by faith, God damn you to hell.

As you can see, Paul was very serious on the importance of maintaining the true gospel of Christ. Let's keep this in mind as we go through Galatians.

In Galatians 1:11–2:10, Paul briefly describes his conversion and apostolic authority as he did not receive the gospel from the apostles. In fact, fourteen years after his conversion, Paul went to the esteemed leaders in Jerusalem and presented them the gospel. James, Cephas, and John, those esteemed as pillars, gave Paul the right hand of fellowship when they recognized the grace that was given to Paul (v. 9). In fact, the apostles added nothing to Paul's gospel (v. 6).

Starting in Galatians 2:11, Paul rebukes Peter for his actions as Peter would draw back and separate from the Gentiles when the circumcision group came. *Drawback* is translated from the original language *hupostelló*. *Hupostelló* means "pulling back to retreat; withdraw; shun; back off, especially due to compromise." Essentially, Peter's compromise to eat with the Judaizers and decline invitations or eating with the Gentiles gave affirmation that he was agreeing with the Judaizer's Mosaic dietary restrictions or other laws such as circumcision. This was throwing other believers such as Barnabas into confusion (2:13). Paul then explodes into proclaiming that man is justified by faith and not by works of the law as he says in Galatians 2:16, "Know that a person is not justified by the works of the law, but by faith in Jesus Christ. So we, too, have put our faith in Christ Jesus that we may be justified by faith in Christ and not by the works of the law, because by the works of the law, no flesh will be justified." Further, he says in Galatians 2:19–21, "For through the law I died to the law so that

I might live for God. I have been crucified with Christ and I no longer live, but Christ lives in me. The life I now live in the body, I live by faith in the Son of God, who love me and gave himself for me. I do not set aside the grace of God, for if righteousness could be gained through the law, Christ died for nothing!"

Paul defends the doctrine of justification by faith and emphatically states that if he sets aside grace that God provides through faith and looks to gain righteousness through the law, then, Christ's grace means nothing. In other words, if you try to rely 1% on your dietary restrictions and 99% on Christ for your salvation, you have proclaimed that Christ died for nothing! Likewise, if you rely 1% on your baptism and confirmation and 99% on Christ for your salvation, you proclaim that Christ died for nothing! If you rely on 1% of your circumcision and 99% on Christ for your salvation, you proclaim that Christ died for nothing! Justifying faith is in Christ alone and no one or nothing else. That is Paul's point.

Paul will go on to ask if the Galatians received the Spirit by works or by faith (v. 2). Clearly, it was by faith. He also cites Abraham being justified by faith (v. 6–9). Paul will go on and state that anyone who relies on the works of the law for salvation are cursed because if you do not continue to do everything written in the Book of the Law, you are under God's curse (v. 10). In verse 11, Paul says, "Clearly no one who relies on the law is justified before God, because "the righteous will live by faith." Additionally, Paul says in verse 14, "He redeemed us in order that the blessing given to Abraham might come to the Gentiles through Christ Jesus, so that by faith we might receive the promise of the Spirit." Paul's point is that justification is not by works, but by faith. In 3:15-22, Paul explains that the law was added for transgressions, which is unlike the promise that was made to Abraham. The law never gave life or could impart life and righteousness never came by the law.

We now transition into the baptism verse in verse 27. However, before we get there, let's take a look at the proceeding verses (v. 23–28):

"Before the coming of this faith, we were held in custody under the law, locked up until the faith that was to come would be revealed. So the law was our guardian until Christ came that we might be justified by faith. Now that this faith has come, we are no longer under a guardian. So in Christ Jesus you are all children of God through faith, for all who were baptized into Christ have clothed yourselves with Christ."

Paul's point remains the same. He is clearly distinguishing between works of the law and faith. Paul's emphasis is that faith is what justifies man before God. In fact, we are all children of God through faith. Verse 26 emphasizes that we are in union with Christ through faith and, then, Paul says that all who were baptized into Christ have been clothed with Christ. Paul is saying that through faith, we are in union with Christ and are children of God. Some scholars have interpreted verse 27 as water baptism being what clothes us with Christ. However, this is a very troublesome interpretation. This completely ignores the doctrine of justification by faith and would put an abrupt stop to Paul's justification doctrine. In fact, just like in Romans 6, Paul would be introducing a justification through baptism abruptly and awkwardly when the golden thread of justification through faith runs through all of Galatians. Additionally, Paul asks the Galatians how they received the Holy Spirit in Galatians 3:1-2 where he says, "O foolish Galatians! Who has bewitched you? It was before your eyes that Jesus Christ was publicly portrayed as crucified. Let me ask you only this: **Did you receive the Spirit by works of the law or by hearing with faith?**" Paul emphasizes this very same point on how someone receives the Holy Spirit where he says in Galatians 3:14, "so that in Christ Jesus the blessing of Abraham might come to the Gentiles, **so that we might receive the promised Spirit through faith.**" Not only in Galatians does

Paul emphasize the Holy Spirit being given through believing the gospel, but he emphasizes this to the Ephesians where he says in Ephesians 1:13, "In him you also, when you **heard the word of truth**, the gospel of your salvation, **and believed in him, were sealed with the promised Holy Spirit**". This verse must be better understood as, since we were justified by faith in Christ, we are baptized or immersed into Christ's perfect work; and, since we are clothed with Christ, we are not only forgiven our sins, we have Christ's imputed righteousness credited to our account. Once again, those who would interpret this passage being water baptism, which accomplishes us being clothed with Christ, would need to contend with the points that have been made:

- Jesus' teaching of regeneration or being born from above (John 3:3)
- Jesus' teaching of being born of water and the Spirit (John 3:5, Ezekiel 36:24–27)
- Nicodemus would not have understood being born of water and the Spirit as Christian baptism as this had not yet been instituted and Jesus was not talking about performing another ritual or sacramental ordinance to enter the kingdom of God. (John 3:5)
- Jesus' teaching on total depravity and flesh only producing flesh and sin (John 3:6)
- Jesus' teaching on the work of the Holy Spirit as being analogous to the wind, which is not controlled, coerced, or commanded (John 3:8)
- Jesus' teaching of the new birth, which is monergistic (John 3:1–10)
- The baptism of repentance for the forgiveness of sins as preached by John the Baptist was a radical call to repentance and not just another ritual. (Luke 3:3–16)
- The baptism of repentance didn't call for just being dipped in, sprinkled with, or immersed in water, but a

heart-searching repentance that elevated sin, brought down pride and self-righteousness, called for acknowledgment that Jews were no better than Gentiles, and called for a complete turning away of one's life in preparation for the Messiah. (Luke 3:3–16)

- Matthew understood that John and all other men could only baptize with water, but Christ could baptize with the Holy Spirit. (Matthew 3:11–12)
- Mark understood that John and all other men could only baptize with water, but Christ could baptize with the Holy Spirit. (Mark 1:8)
- Luke understood that John and all other men could only baptize with water, but Christ could baptize with the Holy Spirit. (Luke 3:16)
- The apostle John understood that John and all other men could only baptize with water, but Christ could baptize with the Holy Spirit. (John 1:31–33)
- John the Baptist understood that he and all other men could only baptize with water, but Christ could baptize with the Holy Spirit. (Matthew 3:11–12, Mark 1:8, Luke 3:16, John 1:31–33)
- Peter understood that he and all other men could only baptize with water, but Christ could baptize with the Holy Spirit. (Acts 2:17–18, 10:44–48, 11:16)
- Jesus understood that only He could baptize with the Holy Spirit and that men could only baptize with water. (Matthew 3:11–12; Mark 1:8; Luke 3:16, 24:49; John 1:31–33, 7:38–39, 14:15–17, 14:26, 15:26, 16:7; Acts 1:4–5, 2:17–18, 10:44–48, 11:16)
- Jesus understood baptism as a work and not baptism as God working through the baptism. (Matthew 3:13–15)
- Paul's understanding of baptism with the Holy Spirit (1 Corinthians 12:13)

- Paul's understanding of the power and position of water baptism in contrast with preaching the gospel (1 Corinthians 1:14–30)
- Paul's understanding of sacraments or signs and seals of faith, which include baptism, and that they had no power to justify man (Romans 4:1–17)

Up to Galatians 3:27, the theme has been justification by faith. Paul goes on to also explain the believer's adoption as God's spiritual children (Galatians 4:5–7). As Paul transitions into chapter 5, his tone gets very serious. In verses 3–4 he says, "Again I declare to every man who lets himself be circumcised that he is obligated to obey the whole law. You who are trying to be justified by the law have been alienated from Christ, you have fallen away from grace." Additionally, in verse 6, he says, "For in Christ Jesus neither circumcision nor uncircumcision has any value. The only thing that counts is faith expressing itself through love." Another way of stating verse 6 could be, "Neither water baptism nor not being water baptized has any value. The only thing that counts is faith expressing itself through love." Paul is very clear here. If anyone is relying on the law for salvation, they are damned and have been cut off from Christ. If anyone is relying on their baptism for salvation, they are damned and cut off from Christ. If anyone is relying on their confirmation for salvation, they are damned and cut off from Christ. Faith in Christ is what matters, not sacraments, not ceremonies, not rituals, not keeping the law, not good works. Faith in Christ is the only thing that will justify man before God. In fact, one that holds to baptismal regeneration is under obligation to keep the whole law which includes Sabbaths, dietary laws, property damage, burnt offerings, grain offerings, sin offerings, guilt offerings, the ordinances of Feasts, tithes, vows, offerings, bodily discharges, and more.

There is another startling statement that Paul makes in verse 12, "As for those agitators, I wish they would go the whole way and emasculate themselves!" Paul is stating that those who would teach circumcision as a means of salvation, he wishes would chop off their genitalia if that would gain God's favor. This could be said of any other means of salvation. These words are inspired by the Holy Spirit. Under the inspiration of the Holy Spirit, Paul wrote this. This is a serious warning to anyone who would teach anything other than being justified by faith in Christ. This is a stern warning for those who teach salvation by works, ceremonies, rituals, rites, sacraments, or law observance.

Lastly, Paul states in Galatians 6:15, "Neither circumcision nor uncircumcision means anything; what counts is the new creation." Likewise, Paul could easily say this, "Neither baptism nor not being baptized means anything; what counts is the new creation" or "Neither confirmation nor not being confirmed means anything; what counts is the new creation." Just as we learned in Romans 6:1–6, if we have union with Christ through faith, we will be a new person with new affections because we have a new heart, a new Spirit, and the Spirit of Christ in us. In fact, let's go back one step further. Unless God the Holy Spirit regenerates us and gives us life, we will never come to repentance and faith. Let us heed Paul's warning of preaching a false gospel and solemnly, humbly, and boldly agree with him that, "God damn any man who preaches a different gospel."

CHAPTER 11

Paul's Understanding of the Washing of Regeneration in Titus

Titus 3:5—He saved us, not on the basis of deeds which we have done in righteousness, but according to His mercy, by the washing of regeneration and renewing by the Holy Spirit.

Like Paul's two letters to Timothy, the apostle gives personal encouragement and counsel to a young pastor who, though well-trained and faithful, faced continuing opposition from ungodly men within the churches where he ministered. Titus was to pass on that encouragement and counsel to the leaders he was to appoint in the Cretan churches. In contrast to several of Paul's other letters, such as those to the churches in Rome and Galatia, the book of Titus does not focus on explaining or defending doctrine. Paul had full confidence in Titus's theological understanding and convictions, evidenced by the fact that he entrusted him with such a demanding ministry. Except for the warning about false teachers and Judaizers, the letter gives no theological correction, strongly suggesting that Paul also had confidence in the doctrinal grounding of most church members there, even though the majority of them were new believers. Doctrines that this epistle affirms include God's sovereign election of believers (1:1–2), His saving grace (2:11; 3:5), Christ's deity and second coming (2:13), Christ's substitutionary atonement (2:14), and the regeneration and renewing of believers by the Holy Spirit (3:5). A good outline for this epistle would include the following:

1. Salutation (1:1–4)
2. Essentials for Effective Evangelism (1:5–3:11)
   a. Among Leaders (1:5–16)
      i. Recognition of Elders (1:5–9)
      ii. Rebuke of False Teachers (1:10–16)
   b. In the Church (2:1–15)
      i. Holy Living (2:1–10)
      ii. Sound Doctrine (2:11–15)
   c. In the World (3:1–11)
      i. Holy Living (3:1–4)
      ii. Sound Doctrine (3:5–11)
3. Conclusion (3:12–14)
4. Benediction (3:15)

With all of this being laid out, and with the previous chapters that have given us a foundation on regeneration, John's baptism of repentance, water baptism, baptism with the Holy Spirit, Paul's understanding of a sacrament's efficacy to save, and going through some of Paul's baptism verses, we should be well equipped to handle Paul's statement on the washing of regeneration. First, let's look at this passage, but starting in Titus 3:3.

Titus 3:3—At one time we too were foolish, disobedient, deceived and enslaved by all kinds of passions and pleasures. We lived in malice and envy, being hated and hating one another.

Paul here is talking about the universal condition of man which is fallen. Paul has stated this condition in Ephesians 2:1–3, Romans 3:10–20, and now here in Titus. Paul is making it abundantly clear that man's default condition is nothing but *fallen and depraved*, meaning man has no innate ability to save himself, but only to sin. He is reminding Titus of this condition.

Titus 3:4–5—But when the kindness and love of God our Savior appeared, he saved us, not because of righteous things we had done, but because of his mercy. He saved us through the washing of rebirth and renewal by the Holy Spirit

Much could be spoken about the kindness and love of God. In fact, in Ephesians 3:18, Paul prays that the Ephesians would go on to know more of the love of God where he says, "May you have power, together with all the Lord's holy people, to grasp how wide and long and high and deep is the love of Christ, and to know this love that surpasses knowledge—that you may be filled to the measure of all the fullness of God."

One of the greatest joys that all the Lord's people will have in eternity is trying to comprehend how much He loves us. We will spend an eternity trying to understand why He would save such a radically depraved group of humans who had no inherent goodness. His great love will be on display as He has proven He loved us from eternity past in His foreknowledge of us, His election of us, His predestination of us, His regeneration of us, His justification of us, His sanctification of us, and His glorification of us. Just as He loved us in eternity past, He will love us into eternity future. Every moment in eternity future, we will see new glories of His love for us. With every song that is sung to the Son of God, we will continue to learn of His love for us. With every new act of kindness and compassion in eternity future, we will continue to see His love for us. In fact, God's love for us will be like a fountain that has no bottom or a book that has no end. The more time spent with God, the more we will have the good pleasure of knowing His love for us. Let's remember God's plan of salvation and how overwhelming it is.

I Stand Amazed
I stand amazed in the presence
Of Jesus the Nazarene
And wonder how He could love me
A sinner, condemned, unclean

How marvelous! How wonderful!
And my song shall ever be
How marvelous! How wonderful!
Is my Savior's love for me!

When with the ransomed in glory
His face I at last shall see
'Twill be my joy through the ages
To sing of His love for me

How marvelous! How wonderful!
And my song shall ever be
How marvelous! How wonderful!
Is my Savior's love for me!

Let's also note that He did not save us because of righteous deeds. The apostle John says it well in John 1:13 where he says, "Children born not of natural descent, nor of human decision or a husband's will, but born of God." No righteous deeds done to us by baptism, no family lineage, no will of any human, no righteous works done by us saved us. God caused us to be born from above and gave us the gift of faith in Christ which justified us.

We then come to verse 5, where Paul says we were saved by the washing of regeneration and renewing by the Holy Spirit. This is often pointed to as a verse that supports baptismal regeneration.

The sacramentalist will say that washing is the water with the Holy Spirit. However, this simply does not work. We've established the following that would not support this washing of regeneration being water baptism just from Paul's theology of water baptism and baptism with the Holy Spirit.

- Paul's understanding of baptism with the Holy Spirit (1 Corinthians 12:13)
- Paul's understanding of the power and position of water baptism in contrast with preaching the gospel (1 Corinthians 1:14–30)
- Paul's understanding of sacraments or signs and seals of faith, which include baptism, and that they had no power to justify man (Romans 4:1–17)

Let's also remember the mountain of Scripture that would need to be explained if this was indeed water baptism:

- Jesus' teaching of regeneration or being born from above (John 3:3)
- Jesus' teaching of being born of water and the Spirit (John 3:5, Ezekiel 36:24–27)
- Nicodemus would not have understood being born of water and the Spirit as Christian baptism as this had not yet been instituted and Jesus was not talking about performing another ritual or sacramental ordinance to enter the kingdom of God. (John 3:5)
- Jesus' teaching on total depravity and flesh only producing flesh and sin (John 3:6)
- Jesus' teaching on the work of the Holy Spirit as being analogous to the wind, which is not controlled, coerced, or commanded (John 3:8)
- Jesus' teaching of the new birth, which is monergistic (John 3:1–10)

- The baptism of repentance for the forgiveness of sins as preached by John the Baptist was a radical call to repentance and not just another ritual. (Luke 3:3–16)
- The baptism of repentance didn't call for just being dipped in, sprinkled with, or immersed in water, but a heart-searching repentance that elevated sin, brought down pride and self-righteousness, called for acknowledgement that Jews were no better than Gentiles, and called for a complete turning away of one's life in preparation for the Messiah. (Luke 3:3–16)
- Matthew understood that John and all other men could only baptize with water, but Christ could baptize with the Holy Spirit. (Matthew 3:11–12)
- Mark understood that John and all other men could only baptize with water, but Christ could baptize with the Holy Spirit. (Mark 1:8)
- Luke understood that John and all other men could only baptize with water, but Christ could baptize with the Holy Spirit. (Luke 3:16)
- The apostle John understood that John and all other men could only baptize with water, but Christ could baptize with the Holy Spirit. (John 1:31–33)
- John the Baptist understood that he and all other men could only baptize with water, but Christ could baptize with the Holy Spirit. (Matthew 3:11–12, Mark 1:8, Luke 3:16, John 1:31–33)
- Peter understood that he and all other men could only baptize with water, but Christ could baptize with the Holy Spirit. (Acts 2:17–18, 10:44–48, 11:16)
- Jesus understood that only He could baptize with the Holy Spirit and that men could only baptize with water. (Matthew 3:11–12; Mark 1:8; Luke 3:16, 24:49; John 1:31–33, 7:38–39, 14:15–17, 14:26, 15:26, 16:7; Acts 1:4–5, 2:17–18, 10:44–48, 11:16)

- Jesus understood baptism as a work and not baptism as God working through the baptism. (Matthew 3:13–15)
- Paul's understanding of baptism with the Holy Spirit (1 Corinthians 12:13)
- Paul's understanding of the power and position of water baptism in contrast with preaching the gospel (1 Corinthians 1:14–30)
- Paul's understanding of sacraments or signs and seals of faith, which include baptism, and that they had no power to justify man (Romans 4:1–17)
- Paul's emphasis that if anyone relies on the law which includes works, rituals, sacraments, and ceremonies that they are alienated from Christ (Galatians 5:3-4)

The word *regeneration* is from *palingenesias,* which is a compound word comprised of *pálin* which means "again" and *genesis* which means "birth, beginning." Properly, *palingenesias* means "born again." As discussed in the first chapter where we discussed regeneration, the word for *born from above* in the original language is *gennethe anothen. Gennethe* is derived from *gennao* which means "to beget, to bring forth" and is used to describe being born. *Anothen* can also be translated as "from above." Putting both words together *born again* can also be translated "born from above." Some translations will translate *gennethe anothen* as "born again or born from above." Paul's use of *born again* in this passage with the word *palingenesias* carries the same meaning. The meaning is that there was a second birth from above that was performed by God the Holy Spirit.

Notice that the second birth occurs by the operating power of the Holy Spirit as he says, "washing of regeneration and renewal by the Holy Spirit." We also learned that this new birth is accomplished by the Holy Spirit as Jesus explains in John 3:6, "Flesh gives birth to flesh, but the Spirit gives birth to spirit." The Holy Spirit is the one who imparts life. Also, notice that Paul also says "renewing," which is *anakainósis* in the original language which means "renewing": a renewal or change of heart and life; properly, a renewal achieved by God's power. This speaks to the work of God bringing forth new life in man. This is the New Covenant promise of Ezekiel 36:26–27, where the LORD says, "Moreover, I will give you a new heart and put a new spirit within you; and I will remove the heart of stone from your flesh and give you a heart of flesh. I will put My Spirit within you and cause you to walk in my statutes, and you will be careful to observe My ordinances." This is the New Covenant promise of Ezekiel 11:19–20, "I will give them an undivided heart and put a new spirit in them; I will remove from them their heart of stone and give them a heart of flesh." This is the New Covenant promise of Jeremiah 31:33–34, "'This is the covenant I will make the people of Israel after that time,' declares the LORD. 'I will put my law in their minds and write it on their hearts. I will be their God, and they will be my people. No longer will they teach their neighbor, or say to one another, "Know the LORD," because they will all know me, from the least of them to the greatest,' declares the LORD. 'For I will forgive their wickedness and will remember their sins no more.'"

Paul is describing the regenerating work of the Holy Spirit in this passage. He is not describing baptismal regeneration as we'll see in Titus 3:6. Let's also note that born from above, born again, or born of God was not something that only Jesus taught. Being born from above is spoken of throughout the Bible. James, the half-brother of Jesus, Peter, the apostle John, and Paul all understood being born from above, born again, or born from God as evidenced by the verses below:

- James 1:18—Of his own will he brought us forth by the word of truth, that we should be a kind of firstfruits of his creatures.

  - *Brought us forth* is from the original word *apokueó,* which means "to give birth or bring forth."
- 1 Peter 1:3—Praise be to the God and Father of our Lord Jesus Christ! In his great mercy he has given us new birth into a living hope through the resurrection of Jesus Christ from the dead.
- 1 Peter 1:23—since you have been born again, not of perishable seed but of imperishable, through the living and abiding word of God
- 1 John 2:29—If you know that he is righteous, you know that everyone who does what is right has been born of him.
- 1 John 3:9—No one who is born of God will continue to sin, because God's seed remains in them; they cannot go on sinning, because they have been born of God.
- 1 John 4:7—Dear friends, let us love one another, for love comes from God. Everyone who loves has been born of God and knows God.
- 1 John 5:1—Everyone who believes that Jesus is the Christ is born of God, and everyone who loves the father loves his child as well.
- 1 John 5:4—For everyone born of God overcomes the world. This is the victory that has overcome the world, even our faith.
- 1 John 5:18—We know that anyone born of God does not continue to sin; the One who was born of God keeps them safe, and the evil one cannot harm them.

Titus 3:6—whom he poured out on us generously through Jesus Christ our Savior

Paul closes the door immediately on this referring to baptismal regeneration. As we have addressed earlier in this book, Jesus is the one who baptizes with the Holy Spirit (salvation) and fire (judgment). The Holy Spirit was given by the Father to the

Son and Christ poured out the Holy Spirit. Who is the one that poured out the Spirit as we learned in Acts 2 and Joel 2? We've learned that it is Jesus who baptizes with the Holy Spirit. Paul fully agrees with Matthew, Mark, Luke, the apostle John, John the Baptist, Jesus, Peter, and the prophet Joel that man baptizes with water, but Jesus baptizes with the Holy Spirit. Paul's statement lines up with the rest of the apostles, prophets, and Christ on regeneration, the new birth, and baptism with the Holy Spirit. God the Holy Spirit regenerates and Jesus baptizes with the Holy Spirit. This passage is not speaking of water baptism. In this section of Scripture, Paul is highlighting the regenerating work of the Holy Spirit in the total salvific work of the baptism with the Holy Spirit.

CHAPTER 12

Peter's "Baptism Now Saves You" Verse

1 Peter 3:21—Corresponding to that, baptism now saves you—not the removal of dirt from the flesh, but an appeal to God for a good conscience—through the resurrection of Jesus Christ.

If ever there was a verse that would support baptismal regeneration it would either be Romans 6:3–4 or 1 Peter 3:21. We have laid a foundation around regeneration, water baptism, baptism with the Holy Spirit, and the efficacy of sacraments to save. So, let's pick up at 1 Peter 3:18 to understand what Peter is stating in the "baptism now saves you" verse.

1 Peter 3:18—For Christ also died for sins once for all, the just for the unjust, so that He might bring us to God, having been put to death in the flesh, but made alive in the Spirit.

This is speaking to Christ's once for all atonement for the sins of His people. *Once for all* is translated from the original word *hapax*. *Hapax* carries the meaning of something done or accomplished that has perpetual validity and never needs repetition. Christ, the sinless Lamb of God who took away the sins of the world, was slain just one time (John 1:29). This is never to be repeated. This sacrifice was sufficient for all the saints of the past to all saints who will be justified in the future. This sacrifice was sufficient for every single sin of all those who would be redeemed. Christ bore our sins on the cross (1 Peter 2:24). Peter is saying that Christ lived in bodily form, Christ died, and Christ was resurrected. Although more could be said about Christ's death on the cross and the meaning of the resurrection, this should suffice for now.

Finally, it says that Christ was made alive in the Spirit. Romans 8:11 says, "God raised Jesus from the dead, and if God's Spirit is living in you, he will also give life to your bodies that die. God is the One who raised Christ from the dead, and he will give life through His Spirit that lives in you." Galatians 1:1 says, "Paul, an apostle (not sent from men nor through the agency of man, but through Jesus Christ and God the Father, who raised Him from the dead)." In John 10:18, Jesus says, "No one has taken it away from Me, but I lay it down on My own initiative. I have authority to lay it down, and I have authority to take it up again. This commandment I received from My Father." What this is saying is that God rose Jesus from the dead. God the Father, God the Son, and God the Holy Spirit were all in agreement. The triune God agreed that Christ's sacrifice was sufficient to pay for the sins of God's people. Let's remember that this speaks to the relationship of the Triune God. The Triune God is one God with three people. All three persons of the Godhead agreed that Christ's work was perfect and sufficient to pay for the sins of His people! The Triune God raised Jesus from the dead!

1 Peter 3:19—In which also He went and made proclamation to the spirits now in prison.

There is debate over where Jesus went. Verse 20 says that these were spirits who were disobedient in the time of Noah. It's very likely that these were fallen angels that were imprisoned, quite possibly in hell and held in chains awaiting their judgment on the last day. Lastly, it says that Jesus made proclamation. The original word is *kérussó,* which as we learned earlier means "to herald or proclaim." It doesn't say that Jesus preached the gospel or *euangelion*. Most likely, Christ was proclaiming His victory over death, the devil, sin, and all authorities to the imprisoned spirits.

1 Peter 3:20—Who once were disobedient, when the patience of God kept waiting in the days of Noah, during the construction of the ark, in which a few, that is, eight persons, were brought safely through the water.

God is a patient God and He was very patient with the wickedness in the time of Noah. In Genesis 3, it says, "Then the LORD said, 'My Spirit will not contend with humans forever, for they are mortal; their days will be a hundred and twenty years,'" and, in verse 5, it says, "The LORD saw how great the wickedness of the human race had become on the earth, and that every inclination of the thoughts of the human heart was only evil all the time." It is a good assumption that God was patient one hundred twenty years as Shem lived five hundred years after the flood (11:11) and Abraham, Ishmael, Isaac, and Jacob all lived to be older than one hundred twenty years (Genesis 25:7; 25:17, 35:28, 47:28). Even Aaron, the first high priest of Israel, who lived approximately a thousand years after the Flood, lived to be one hundred twenty-three years (Numbers 33:39). Noah was a preacher of righteousness for one hundred twenty years before the commencement of the Flood. God gave the people one hundred twenty years of preaching through Noah before He initiated the Flood. Behold the patience of God!

In 2 Peter 2:25, it says, "and did not spare the ancient world, but protected Noah, a preacher of righteousness, with seven others, when He brought a flood upon the world of the ungodly," and in Hebrews 11:7, it says, "By faith Noah, being warned by God about things not yet seen, in reverence prepared an ark for the salvation of his household, by which he condemned the world, and became an heir of the righteousness which is according to faith." Noah had warned the ungodly of the looming disaster, but no one would listen except his three sons, their wives, and Noah's wife (Genesis 7:7). Some estimate that the world population could have been in the millions or possibly billions. It's important not to derail explaining 1 Peter 3:21. However, God's wrath, justice, mercy, and kindness were all on display in the Flood. His wrath and justice were on display in punishing sin, and His mercy and kindness in sparing humanity. Let us never forget that God is love (1 John 4:8); but, since God is love, He must also hate that which is wicked (John 3:36).

One of the most important and key phrases to help understand verse 21 is the last part of verse 20 which says, "Eight persons were brought safely through the water." You will notice in verse 21 that Peter is not talking about the saving effects of water because water was the agent of destruction. No, when Peter explains "baptism now saves you," he is making an analogy to the eight persons that were in the boat and rescued through the boat. This is extremely important in understanding verse 21.

1 Peter 3:21—Corresponding to that, baptism now saves you—not the removal of dirt from the flesh, but an appeal to God for a good conscience—through the resurrection of Jesus Christ.

Peter will now explain how the flood and the ark correspond to baptism. The word *corresponding* is translated from the original word which is *antitupos*. *Antitupos* can also mean an antitype which corresponds to (fulfills) a type (a predictive symbol). Peter will now explain how the flood corresponds to baptism in a saving way. He immediately starts off and says, "Not the removal of dirt from the flesh." It's as if Peter is saying, "Wait. Hold on. I'm not talking about the sacrament of baptism which removes filth from the flesh." Although Peter says baptism now saves you, his next statement immediately opposes talking about water baptism saving. Additionally, as we mentioned in verse 20, the water in the Flood was used as the agent of destruction and was not the saving agent. Therefore, the water would not carry the meaning of washing away of sins or the regenerating work of the Holy Spirit. What Peter is saying is that just as the eight persons went into the boat and were rescued, baptism symbolizes the appeal the sinner makes to God for a good conscience through Jesus Christ.

In other words, just as Noah escaped the wrath of God through the boat, so we can escape the wrath of God through faith in Jesus Christ as Jesus took the wrath of God upon Himself and Jesus is our refuge in judgment. Through faith in Christ, we escape the wrath to come (1 Thessalonians 1:10). Not only is Peter saying that the appeal for a good conscience comes through Jesus Christ, but he also explains why it comes through Jesus Christ in verse 22 where Jesus is at the right hand of God and is in heaven, with all power and authority. This speaks to the sinner appealing to Christ, knowing they are a sinner, knowing they deserve the wrath of God, repenting of sin, and putting faith in Christ who has already taken the wrath and judgment of His people. of His people. Peter is emphasizing that since Jesus was able to take the wrath of God and is resurrected and ascended, so those who come to Christ in saving faith can be assured that they will be sheltered from the wrath God by Jesus Christ who suffered the wrath of God on the cross and was also able to raise himself from the dead and ascend into heaven afterwards. Essentially, we should see Jesus as the ark that can survive the wrath of God and the only appeal that can be made to avoid the wrath of God must be made through faith in Jesus Christ who is able to bring us safely through the wrath of God and judgment. Jesus has all authority in heaven and on earth to save and judge as He is equal with the Father. This is what Peter is saying. Peter is not arguing for baptismal regeneration. This would not be consistent with his antitype of Noah's family entering the ark to escape the Flood. Baptismal regeneration would also not be appropriate as Peter clarifies that it's "not the removal of dirt from the flesh." Lastly, the appeal to a good conscience should be understood as the sinner coming to faith in Christ and taking refuge in Christ alone to escape the wrath to come (1 Thessalonians 1:10). Peter makes this abundantly clear earlier on in his epistle:

- 1 Peter 1:3–5—Praise be to God and Father of our Lord Jesus Christ! In his great mercy he has given us new birth into a living hope through the resurrection of Jesus Christ from the dead, and into an inheritance that can never perish, spoil, or fade. This inheritance is kept in heaven for you, who through **faith** are shielded by God's power until the coming of the salvation that is ready to be revealed in the last time.
- 1 Peter 1:6–7—In all this you greatly rejoice, though now for a little while you may have had to suffer grief in all kinds of trials. These have come so that the proven genuineness of your **faith**—of greater worth than gold, which perishes even though refined by fire—may result in praise, glory, and honor when Jesus Christ is revealed.
- 1 Peter 1:8—Though you have not seen him, you love him; and even though you do not see him now, you believe in him and are filled with an inexpressible and glorious joy.
- 1 Peter 1:9—for you are receiving the end result of your **faith**, the salvation of your souls

It's very important to read these verses in context to understand Peter's argument of how baptism correlates to Noah being rescued from the Flood by the ark. Rendering a proper understanding of this passage shows that water baptism being a means for salvation is not what Peter is talking about. Peter's antitype was that just as Noah was shielded from the Flood through the ark, so we who put our faith in Christ are shielded from the wrath and judgment to come. Faith in Christ is what saves, not water baptism.

Chapter 13

The Doctrine of Baptism and Regeneration According to The Lutheran Church—Missouri Synod

It would be erroneous to visit a few LCMS churches and conclude that what has happened in a cluster of churches applies to all other LCMS churches. Therefore, it is best to review and understand the LCMS's teaching and position on baptismal regeneration. This can be done by reviewing *Luther's Small and Large Catechisms*. Some texts of *Luther's Small and Large Catechisms* have been set in bold to highlight important points in the LCMS's baptismal regeneration doctrine.

From *Luther's Small Catechism* (1)

The Sacrament of Holy Baptism

- What benefits does baptism give?
  - **It works forgiveness of sins, rescues from death and the devil, and gives eternal salvation to all who believe this**, as the words and promises of God declare.

- Which are these words and promises of God
  - Christ our Lord says in the last Chapter of Mark: "Whoever believes and is baptized will be saved, but whoever does not believe will be condemned." (Mark 16:16)
- How can water do such great things?
  - **Certainly not just water, but the word of God in and with the water does these things, along with the faith which trust this word of God in the water. For without God's word the water is plain water and no Baptism. But with the word of God it is a Baptism, that is, a life-giving water, rich in grace, and a washing of the new birth in the Holy Spirit**, as St. Paul says in Titus, chapter 3: "He saved us through the washing of rebirth and renewal by the Holy Spirit, whom He poured out on us generously through Jesus Christ our Savior, so that, having been justified by His grace, we might become heirs having the hope of eternal life. This is a trust-worthy saying." (Titus 3:5–8)
- What does such baptizing with water indicate?
  - It indicates that the old Adam in us should by daily contrition and repentance be drowned and die with all sins and evil desires, and that a new man should daily emerge and arise to live before God in righteousness and purity forever.
- Where is this written?
  - St Paul writes in Romans chapter 6: "We were therefore buried with Him through baptism into death in order that, just as Christ was raised from the dead through the glory of the Father, we too may live a new life." (Romans 6:4)

The Blessings of Baptism

- 248. **What great and precious things are given in Baptism?**
  - A. **Forgiveness of Sins**
    - Acts 2:38—Repent and be baptized, every one of you, in the name of Jesus Christ for the forgiveness of your sins.
    - Acts 22:16—Get up, be baptized and wash your sins away.
  - B. **Rescues from Death and the Devil**
    - Romans 6:3, 5—Don't you know that all of us who were baptized into Christ Jesus were baptized into His death? . . . If we have been united with Him like this in His death, we will certainly also be united with Him in His resurrection.
    - Galatians 3:27—All of you who were baptized into Christ have clothed yourselves with Christ.
    - Colossians 1:13–14—He has rescued us from the dominion of darkness and brought us into the kingdom of the Son He loves, in whom we have redemption, the forgiveness of sins.
  - C. **Gives Eternal Salvation**
    - Mark 16:16 Whoever believes and is baptized will be saved
    - 1 Peter 3:21 This water [of Noah's flood] symbolizes baptism that now saves you also... It saves you by the resurrection of Jesus Christ.
    - Titus 3:5 He saved us through the washing of rebirth and renewal by the Holy Spirit
- 252. Why are we not to seek a "baptism with the Holy Spirit" in addition to the Sacrament of Holy Baptism?
  - B. The sacrament is not a water-only or a Spirit-only baptism, but a water-and-Spirit Baptism

- John 3:5—No one can enter the kingdom of God unless he is born of water and the Spirit.
- Titus 3:5—He saves us through the washing of rebirth and renewal by the Holy Spirit.

The Power of Baptism

- 253. **How does baptismal water work forgiveness of sins, rescue from death and the devil, and give eternal salvation?**
    - **God's words of institution put these great blessings into Baptism. Faith, which trust this word of God in the water, takes the blessings out and makes them our own.**
        - Ephesians 5:26—Christ loves the church and gave Himself up for her to make her holy, cleansing her by the washing with water through the word.
        - Galatians 3:26–27—You are all sons of God through faith in Christ Jesus, for all of you who were baptized into Christ have clothed yourselves with Christ.
- 260. With which words do we regularly remember our Baptism?
    - **The words "in the name of the Father, and of the Son, and of the Holy Spirit" come from the baptismal command (Matthew 28:19) and are known as the Trinitarian Invocation. By repeating these words, in church or by ourselves, we recall, claim, and confess before heaven, earth, and hell all that God the Holy Trinity has given us in our Baptism.**

There is no doubt that from *Luther's Small Catechism*, one is taught or catechized that baptism works forgiveness of sins, rescues from death and the devil, and gives eternal salvation. It is also taught that baptism is not just a water baptism, but a water-and-spirit baptism which uses John 3:5 and Titus 3:5 as supporting verses.

***Luther's Large Catechism* on Infant Baptism (2)**

47 Here a question occurs by which the devil, through his sects, confuses the world, namely, of infant baptism, whether children also believe, and are justly baptized. Concerning this we say briefly:

48 Let the simple dismiss this question from their minds, and refer it to the learned. But if you wish to answer,

49 then answer thus:

That the baptism of infants is pleasing to Christ is sufficiently proved from His own work, namely, **that God sanctifies many of them who have been thus baptized, and has given them the Holy Ghost**; and that there are yet many even to-day in whom we perceive that they have the Holy Ghost both because of their doctrine and life; as it is also given to us by the grace of God that we can explain the Scriptures and come to the knowledge of Christ, which is impossible without the Holy Ghost.

50 But if God did not accept the baptism of infants, He would not give the Holy Ghost nor any of His gifts to any of them; in short, during this long time unto this day no man upon earth could have been a Christian. Now, since God confirms Baptism by the gifts of His Holy Ghost, as is plainly perceptible in some of the church fathers, as St Bernard, Gerson, John Hus, and others, who were baptized in infancy, and since the holy Christian Church cannot perish until the end of the world, they must acknowledge that such infant baptism is pleasing to God. For He can never be opposed to Himself, or support falsehood and wickedness, or for its promotion impart His grace and Spirit.

51 This is indeed the best and strongest proof for the simple-minded and unlearned. For they shall not take from us or overthrow this article: I believe a holy Christian Church, the communion of saints.

52 **Further, we say that we are not so much concerned to know whether the person baptized believes or not; for on that account Baptism does not become invalid; but everything depends upon the Word and command of God.**

53 This now is perhaps somewhat acute, but it rests entirely upon what I have said, **that Baptism is nothing else than water and the Word of God in and with each other, that is, when the Word is added to the water, Baptism is valid, even though faith be wanting.** For my faith does not make Baptism, but receives it. **Now, Baptism does not become invalid even though it be wrongly received or employed; since it is not bound (as stated) to our faith, but to the Word.**

54 **For even though a Jew should to-day come dishonestly and with evil purpose, and we should baptize him in all good faith, we must say that his baptism is nevertheless genuine. For here is the water together with the Word of God, even though he does not receive it as he should, just as those who unworthily go to the Sacrament receive the true Sacrament, even though they do not believe.**

55 Thus you see that the objection of the sectarians is vain. For (as we have said) even though infants did not believe, which, however, is not the case, yet their baptism as now shown would be valid, and no one should rebaptize them; just as nothing is detracted from the Sacrament though some one approach it with evil purpose, and he could not be allowed on account of his abuse to take it a second time the selfsame hour, as though he had not received the true Sacrament at first; for that would mean to blaspheme and profane the Sacrament in the worst manner. How dare we think that God's Word and ordinance should be wrong and invalid because we make a wrong use of it?

56 Therefore I say, if you did not believe then believe now and say thus: The baptism indeed was right, but I, alas! did not receive it aright. For I myself also, and all who are baptized, must speak thus before God: I come hither in my faith and in that of others,

yet I cannot rest in this, that I believe, and that many people pray for me; but in this I rest, that it is Thy Word and command. Just as I go to the Sacrament trusting not in my faith, but in the Word of Christ; whether I am strong or weak, that I commit to God. But this I know, that He bids me go, eat and drink, etc., and gives me His body and blood; that will not deceive me or prove false to me.

57 Thus we do also in infant baptism. **We bring the child in the conviction and hope that it believes, and we pray that God may grant it faith; but we do not baptize it upon that, but solely upon the command of God.** Why so? Because we know that God does not lie. I and my neighbor and, in short, all men, may err and deceive, but the Word of God cannot err.

58 Therefore they are presumptuous, clumsy minds that draw such inferences and conclusions as these: **Where there is not the true faith, there also can be no true Baptism**. Just as if I would infer: If I do not believe, then Christ is nothing; or thus: If I am not obedient, then father, mother, and government are nothing. Is that a correct conclusion, that whenever any one does not do what he ought, the thing in itself shall be nothing and of no value?

59 My dear, just invert the argument and rather draw this inference: **For this very reason Baptism is something and is right, because it has been wrongly received**. For if it were not right and true in itself, it could not be misused nor sinned against. The saying is: *Abusus non tollit, sed confirmat substantiam*, Abuse does not destroy the essence, but confirms it. **For gold is not the less gold though a harlot wear it in sin and shame.**

60 **Therefore let it be decided that Baptism always remains true, retains its full essence, even though a single person should be baptized, and he, in addition, should not believe truly**. For God's ordinance and Word cannot be made variable or be altered by men.

[61] But these people, the fanatics, are so blinded that they do not see the Word and command of God, and regard Baptism and the magistrates only as they regard water in the brook or in pots, or as any other man; and because they do not see faith nor obedience, they conclude that they are to be regarded as invalid.

[62] Here lurks a concealed seditious devil, who would like to tear the crown from the head of authority and then trample it under foot, and, in addition, pervert and bring to naught all the works and ordinances of God.

[63] **Therefore we must be watchful and well-armed, and not allow ourselves to be directed nor turned away from the Word, in order that we may not regard Baptism as a mere empty sign, as the fanatics dream.**

[64] Lastly, we must also know what Baptism signifies, and why God has ordained just such external sign and ceremony for the Sacrament by which we are first received into the Christian Church.

[65] But the act or ceremony is this, that we are sunk under the water, which passes over us, and afterwards are drawn out again. **These two parts, to be sunk under the water and drawn out again, signify the power and operation of Baptism, which is nothing else than putting to death the old Adam, and after that the resurrection of the new man, both of which must take place in us all our lives, so that a truly Christian life is nothing else than a daily baptism, once begun and ever to be continued.** For this must be practised without ceasing, that we ever keep purging away whatever is of the old Adam, and that that which belongs to the new man come forth.

[66] But what is the old man? It is that which is born in us from Adam, angry, hateful, envious, unchaste, stingy, lazy, haughty, yea, unbelieving, infected with all vices, and having by nature nothing good in it.

[67] Now, when we are come into the kingdom of Christ, these things must daily decrease, that the longer we live we become

more gentle, more patient, more meek, and ever withdraw more and more from unbelief, avarice, hatred, envy, haughtiness.

[68] This is the true use of Baptism among Christians, as signified by baptizing with water. Where this, therefore, is not practised, but the old man is left unbridled, so as to continually become stronger, that is not using Baptism, but striving against Baptism.

[69] For those who are without Christ cannot but daily become worse, according to the proverb which expresses the truth, "Worse and worse—the longer, the worse."

[70] If a year ago one was proud and avaricious, then he is much prouder and more avaricious this year, so that the vice grows and increases with him from his youth up. A young child has no special vice; but when it grows up, it becomes unchaste and impure, and when it reaches maturity, real vices begin to prevail the longer, the more.

[71] **Therefore the old man goes unrestrained in his nature if he is not checked and suppressed by the power of Baptism. On the other hand, where men have become Christians, he daily decreases until he finally perishes. That is truly to be buried in Baptism, and daily to come forth again.**

[72] Therefore the external sign is appointed not only for a powerful effect, but also for a signification.

[73] Where, therefore, faith flourishes with its fruits, there it has no empty signification, but the work [of mortifying the flesh] accompanies it; but where faith is wanting, it remains a mere unfruitful sign.

[74] And here you see that Baptism, both in its power and signification, comprehends also the third Sacrament, which has been called repentance,

[75] **as it is really nothing else than Baptism. For what else is repentance but an earnest attack upon the old man [that his lusts be restrained] and entering upon a new life? Therefore, if you live in repentance, you walk in Baptism,** which not only

signifies such a new life, but also produces, begins, and exercises it.

76 **For therein are given grace, the Spirit, and power to suppress the old man**, so that the new man may come forth and become strong.

77 **Therefore our Baptism abides forever; and even though some one should fall from it and sin, nevertheless we always have access thereto, that we may again subdue the old man.**

78 But we need not again be sprinkled with water; for though we were put under the water a hundred times, it would nevertheless be only one Baptism, although the operation and signification continue and remain.

79 **Repentance, therefore, is nothing else than a return and approach to Baptism, that we repeat and practise what we began before**, but abandoned.

80 This I say lest we fall into the opinion in which we were for a long time, imagining that our Baptism is something past, which we can no longer use after we have fallen again into sin. The reason is, that it is regarded only according to the external act once performed [and completed].

81 And this arose from the fact that St Jerome wrote that repentance is the second plank by which we must swim forth and cross over after the ship is broken, on which we step and are carried across when we come into the Christian Church.

82 Thereby the use of Baptism has been abolished so that it can profit us no longer. Therefore the statement is not correct, or at any rate not rightly understood. For the ship never breaks, because (as we have said) it is the ordinance of God, and not a work of ours; but it happens, indeed, that we slip and fall out of the ship. Yet if any one fall out, let him see to it that he swim up and cling to it till he again come into it and live in it, as he had formerly begun.

83 **Thus it appears what a great, excellent thing Baptism is, which delivers us from the jaws of the devil and makes us God's**

own, suppresses and takes away sin, and then daily strengthens the new man; and is and remains ever efficacious until we pass from this estate of misery to eternal glory.

[84] For this reason let every one esteem his Baptism as a daily dress in which he is to walk constantly, that he may ever be found in the faith and its fruits, that he suppress the old man and grow up in the new.

[85] For if we would be Christians, we must practise the work whereby we are Christians.

[86] **But if any one fall away from it, let him again come into it. For just as Christ, the Mercy-seat, does not recede from us or forbid us to come to Him again, even though we sin, so all His treasure and gifts also remain. If, therefore, we have once in Baptism obtained forgiveness of sin, it will remain every day, as long as we live, that is, as long as we carry the old man about our neck.**

Summarizing Luther's position on infant baptism in *Luther's Large Catechism* can be quite difficult, but here is what can be gathered from Luther's statements that come from *Luther's Large Catechism*:

- In baptism, God sanctifies and gives the Holy Spirit. (49)
- The Word of God and water are what make baptism valid. (52, 53)
- Baptism is efficacious and effective because of the Word of God in and with the water. (53)
- Baptism is genuine even for the Christ denying, unbelieving individual. (54)
- There is hope that the child believes and the hope that God grants faith, but baptism is based off of God's command. (57)
- Baptism retains its full essence and effectiveness even if someone does not truly believe. (60)
- Baptism is more than a sign. (63)

- A true baptism is one where there is a drowning of the old Adam. (65)
- Repentance is the third sacrament and that walking in repentance is walking in baptism. (75)
- In baptism, you are given the Holy Spirit to suppress the old Adam and the new man comes forth. (76)
- Repentance is a return to baptism and baptism lasts forever. (77, 79)
- Baptism saves from the devil, makes you a child of God, suppresses sin, takes away sin (forgiveness), strengthens the new man, and is efficacious until death. (83)
- Baptism remains forever, only as long as one carries it around his neck. (86)

While it appears that Luther's view on baptism varied from being effective when the water and God's Word were combined to hoping that a child would believe and God would grant him faith, *Luther's Small Catechism* makes no such doubt or claim on the efficacy of baptism to save. In fact, *Luther's Small Catechism* explains that baptism forgives sins, rescues from death and the devil, and gives eternal life because God's Word and faith are placed in the water. This is a very clear teaching by the LCMS that the sacrament of Baptism saves.

Luther also goes on to say, "Now, they are so mad as to separate faith and that to which faith clings and is bound though it be something external. Yea, it shall and must be something external, that it may be apprehended by the senses, and understood and thereby be brought into the heart, as indeed the entire Gospel is an external, verbal preaching." Additionally, he says of baptism, "Thus faith clings to the water, and believes that it is Baptism, in which there is pure salvation and life; not through the water (as we have sufficiently stated), but through the fact that it is embodied in the Word and institution of God, and the name of God inheres in it. Now, if I believe this, what else is it than believing in God as in Him who has given and planted His Word into this ordinance, and proposes to us this external thing wherein we may apprehend such a treasure?" Martin Luther makes a difficult statement here saying that believing in the baptism is the same as believing in God as the Word has been planted into the ordinance of baptism. This is quite difficult to understand, but Luther seems to say that believing in your baptism is the same as believing in God as the Word is in the water.

Martin Luther also taught of Baptism that it was not man's work, but God's work where he says, "Baptism, however, is not our work, but God's (for, as was stated, you must put Christ-baptism far away from a bath-keeper's baptism). God's works, however are saving and necessary for salvation, and do not exclude, but demand, faith; for without faith they could not be apprehended. For by suffering the water to be poured upon you, you have not yet received Baptism in such a manner that it benefits you anything; but it becomes beneficial to you if you have yourself baptized with the thought that this is according to God's command and ordinance, and besides in God's name, in order that you may receive in the water the promised salvation. Now, this the fist cannot do, nor the body; but the heart must believe it." Luther's statement here seems to go on to further clarify that baptism becomes beneficial or salvation producing to one if one thinks or believes that the baptism is according to God's command and ordinance with God's name.

Luther's view on baptism includes many thoughts and perspectives that can be difficult to comprehend. On the one hand, baptism is water and the Word which makes a baptism. On the other hand, faith must cling to the external element. On the other hand, baptism is beneficial to those baptized if you believe it's according to God's command and ordinance and in God's name. However, in Luther's final analysis he goes on saying, "Thus we must regard Baptism and make it profitable to ourselves, that when our sins and conscience oppress us, we strengthen ourselves and take comfort and say: Nevertheless I am baptized; but if I am baptized, it is promised me that I shall be saved and have eternal life, both in soul and body."

The doctrine of baptism in the LCMS does become quite confusing in the machinations of how baptism works with water, faith, the Word, and the command being in and with the water. However, the LCMS teaches the sacrament of baptism gives forgiveness of sins and eternal life. In fact, Luther's statement is quite ominous that when our sins and conscience oppress us, we would look to our baptism as confidence that we have eternal life. He makes an incredibly disturbing statement that one can look to their baptism as the hope of eternal life. For all the good that Luther did, it is a sad and unbelievably disastrous position that he took on baptism. To cling to baptism in the New Covenant as a means of salvation is just as disastrous as clinging to circumcision in the Old Covenant as a means of salvation.

CHAPTER 14

The Narrow Gate

Matthew 7:13–14—Enter through the narrow gate; for the gate is wide and the way is broad that leads to destruction, and there are many who enter through it. For the gate is small and the way is narrow that leads to life, and there are few who find it.

The Sermon on the Mount covers the character and attitudes of people who are in the kingdom of heaven, sets forth the true standard of the law which cannot be achieved by man, attacks superficial works and worship and contrasts them with true spiritual works and worship, calls for the priority and preeminence of the kingdom of heaven, and warns listeners to go through the narrow gate and enter the kingdom of heaven.

As Jesus concludes His Sermon on the Mount, He starts making black and white distinctions for His audience. He will state that there is a narrow gate and a wide gate (Matthew 7:13). He will state that there is a narrow way and a broad way (Matthew 7:13–14). He will state that it will be hard to find the narrow gate and enter it because of false prophets and false teachers (Matthew 7:15–20). Jesus states that there are going to be false disciples who will make it difficult as well and there is danger in making a profession of faith with no possession of saving faith (Matthew 7:21–23). Finally, Jesus states that there are two foundations and two ways to listen (Matthew 7:24–27). We will start in Matthew 7:13–14 to see Jesus' exhortation to enter through the narrow gate.

First, in verse 13, let's notice that Jesus is giving a command. Jesus is saying you must enter through the narrow gate. This entrance into the narrow gate is not passive. It's clear that we are saved by grace, through faith, in Christ (Ephesians 2:8–9). However, the free gift of grace by faith never operates outside of man's intellect, emotions, and volition. It's not enough to look at the gate, admire the gate, and think nice thoughts about the gate. No, you must enter through it! Isaiah captures this truth of the free gift of faith which has a volitional component in Isaiah 55:1, where he says, "Come, all you who are thirsty, come to the waters; and you who have no money, come, buy and eat! Come buy wine and milk without money and without cost." Notice that it's all free and costs nothing, but there is still the volitional component to come, buy, and eat. So, it is with the narrow gate. Entering the narrow gate is a command. There's nothing you can do to buy your way to get through the narrow gate but entering through the narrow gate always has an intellectual, emotional, and volitional component to it. Saving faith is never void of intellect, emotion, and volition.

Second, let's notice that entrance through the narrow gate is a struggle. In fact, in Luke 13:22, Jesus says, "Strive to enter through the narrow door; for many, I tell you, will seek to enter and will not be able." The word *strive* is translated from the original word *agónizomai*, which means "to struggle or to strive (as in an athletic contest or warfare)." Also note in Luke 13:24 that many will seek to enter but will not be able. Entering this gate is not going to be easy. Entering through this gate will take effort. In fact, in Matthew 11:12, Jesus says these words, "And from the days of John the Baptist until now the kingdom of heaven has been treated violently, and violent men take it by force." Jesus isn't saying that you must be a violent person to enter. No, he's saying that entering the kingdom of heaven is a struggle and those that struggle violently are those that enter. Once again, this is not a works-based salvation, but Jesus is indicating that entering the kingdom of heaven is far from a passive entrance. As we'll see later, the call to enter requires repentance, denial of self, cross bearing, and submission and trust in Christ alone. These are the words of Christ Himself that proclaim that this entry will be agonizing, and we'll speak of this more later.

Third, let's note the definite article *the* narrow gate. It is a definite article and not an indefinite article of *a* or *an*. There is one narrow gate and that is Jesus Christ. In John 10:7,9 Jesus says, "Truly, truly I say to you, I am the door of the sheep." And "I am the door; if anyone enters through Me, he will be saved, and will go in and out and find pasture." There is but one narrow gate. There is only one broad gate as well.

Fourth, let's note that "the" gate is narrow. The word *narrow* is translated from the original word which is *stenos*. You hear the English word *stenosis* derived from this. It's important to note that the gate is narrow in that this is a gate that doesn't allow the passage of many people at one time. No, this gate needs to be entered individually. This gate needs to be sought after and entered by one person at a time. Note that Jesus is speaking to the people that this is a personal decision. He doesn't say, "You can enter based on someone else's merits. You can enter with your mom. You can enter with your dad. You can enter because of your last name." No, this gate must be entered by just you and purposefully. In fact, when Jesus says the gate is narrow, He is giving the idea that you will not run through it. You will not be able to take all your sin and personal agenda with you. Entering this gate will strip you of everything. We'll look to Matthew 5:3–6 to explain this more.

Fifth, let's note that we must enter this gate urgently because the broad gate and the broad road are connected which leads to destruction. Jesus is telling us that this is an urgent matter. You need to go through this narrow gate right now. Otherwise, you're headed towards hell and destruction. This is not a decision that you should wait on. As James 4:14 says, "Yet you do not know what your life will be like tomorrow. For you are just a vapor that appears for a little while, and then vanishes away." You must deal earnestly and urgently with God for your eternal future rides on entering this narrow gate.

Sixth, let's note that the gate is wide. *Wide* has been translated from the original word *platus*. The word *platus* means "to be broad like a street." The wide gate isn't necessarily just talking about the false religions of Islam, Buddhism, Taoism, Confucianism, Taoism, Shintoism, agnosticism, universalism, and any other "ism" religion that exists. No, this could also include the false Christs of the Jehovah Witnesses and the Mormons. Let's be even more specific. This wide gate also includes the false gospels of Roman Catholicism, which include faith plus works being needed for salvation. This wide gate also includes the false gospel of the LCMS, which says that water baptism saves. This wide gate also includes "easy believism" which allows for just mental assent to the facts of the gospel.

Seventh, let's note that the wide gate gives way to the broad way. *Broad* is translated from the original word which is *euruchóros*. The word *euruchóros* means "broad, spacious, wide." This broad road talks to one's lifestyle or manner of walking. This broad road allows one to live their life any way they want. This broad road allows for antinomianism or antilaw. This broad road allows for spiritual apathy towards Christ. This broad road requires no cross carrying, no self-denial, no submission, no following. This broad road is broad because it is not confined to living under God's Word.

Eighth, let's note that the wide road which gives way to destruction. Entering through the broad gate and walking the broad way leads to hell. This broad gate and broad road leads to the unquenchable fire (Matthew 3:12). This broad gate and wide road lead to an eternal destiny that will be worse than the burning sulfur which rained down on Sodom and Gomorrah (Genesis 19:24, Matthew 11:24). This broad gate and wide road will lead into outer darkness where there will be weeping and gnashing of teeth (Matthew 25:30). The broad gate and wide road will lead to the lake of fire (Revelation 20:14–15). The broad gate and wide road will lead to receiving eternal torment (Luke 12:47). The broad gate and wide road will lead to a fire that cannot be escaped (Luke 16:25–26).

Ninth, let's note that many enter through the wide gate. Jesus says that there are many that enter through the broad gate that leads to destruction (Matthew 7:13). The word *many* comes from the original word *polus*. *Polus* means "much, many, high in number, multitudinous, great in amount." This is a somber statement. In God's sovereign and omniscient wisdom, He has so determined that a vast multitude will go to hell. A large amount of humanity will suffer the wrath of God in hell. Multitudes will spend the rest of eternity burning in fire. There will be many that never repent. There will be many that never came in a saving way to Christ. I don't know if this point can be overemphasized. Does it not break your heart that many of your loved ones are headed towards eternal destruction? Does it not break your heart that they do not have Christ? Does it break your heart that many are self-deceived in false religion including false "Christian" churches? Do you have a heart for the lost like the Good Shepherd? Do you wish to seek to tell people how to enter through the narrow gate? Does it bother you when a false gospel is preached that leads people to hell?

Tenth, let's note that the road is narrow that leads to life. The word *narrow* comes from the original word *thlibó* which means "to press, afflict, or properly to rub together to constrict." It also gives the idea that it's a road of affliction or persecution. Think of rubbing your index finger and your thumb together. This is the sense in which this word is used. It is tight. It is pressed together. It is narrow. It is a road of persecution. The way is narrow because one's life is lived according to God's Word. God calls His saints to be holy. Not perfect, but holy and set apart. God has good works foreordained for His people (Ephesians 2:10). God's purpose is to have His saints stand out as a salt and light (Matthew 5:14). God desires His people to bear much fruit (John 15:8). God desires His people to be holy (1 Peter 1:16). God has removed the heart of stone from all those who have entered the narrow gate and given them a heart of flesh, a new spirit, and the Holy Spirit to be able to follow His statutes (Ezekiel 36:25–27). God will have written His law on the minds and hearts of all of those who enter the narrow gate. God will teach them to know Him so they can walk the narrow road (Hebrews 8:10–11). All those who enter the narrow gate, and thus enter into the New Covenant, will have fear of the Lord, and singleness of heart and action, so that they will never turn away from Him (Jeremiah 32:38–40).

Eleventh, note that there are few who find that narrow gate and narrow road. Jesus says, "But small is the gate and narrow the road that leads to life, and only a few find it." *Few* is translated from the original word which is *oligos*. *Oligos* means "few, little, or small." Jesus is not saying that heaven will be scarcely populated but is emphasizing that a great majority of the people will not find saving faith in Christ.

Twelfth, let's note that the narrow gate leads to the narrow road. In other words, when one is justified, he is placed on the narrow road. He does not enter the narrow gate, then go on the broad road and then later decide to walk the narrow road. No, when someone enters the narrow gate, they are immediately placed on the narrow road. After justification, sanctification immediately follows. This speaks not to the perfection of one's walk as a Christian, but rather, an immediate change in their walk of life that will grow in conformance to God's Word and the image of His Son as Romans 8:29–30 says, "For those God foreknew he also predestined to be confirmed to the image of his Son, that he might be the firstborn among many brothers and sisters. And those he predestined, he also called; those he called, he also justified; those he justified, he also glorified."

Thirteenth, let's note that the gate is hard to find. It's not only agonizing and difficult to go through, but on top of that, it's hard to find as Jesus says, "There are few who find it." As stated previously, the broad gate not only includes the false religions of the world, but also includes false Christianity. In just two verses, Jesus is warning all generations to be diligent to find the narrow gate, count the costs of walking the narrow road, and then agonize to enter through the narrow gate for few are those who find it.

The False Teachers and False Prophets Will Make the Narrow Gate Hard to Find

Matthew 7:15–20—Beware of the false prophets, who come to you in sheep's clothing, but inwardly are ravenous wolves. You will know them by their fruits. Grapes are not gathered from thorn bushes, nor figs from thistles, are they? So every good tree bears good fruit, but the bad tree bears bad fruit. A good tree cannot bear bad fruit, nor can a bad tree bear good fruit. Every tree that does not bear good fruit is cut down and thrown into the fire. So then, you will know them by their fruits.

Jesus gives these warnings for all generations to beware and be on the lookout for false teachers. He adds that entering the narrow gate is hard because of the false prophets in the world. Keep in mind that Jesus is talking to religious people. He's not talking to atheists or those who worship false gods. No, He is talking to

Jews in this message. Jesus is saying that entering through the narrow gate is going to be extremely hard because there are going to be false teachers who are disguised as shepherds and sheep but will ultimately lead those who follow them astray.

It will be difficult to find the narrow gate because there will be false prophets that come from large seminaries and have advanced degrees from institutions that are called "Christian" but teach lies that send people to hell. It will be difficult to find the narrow gate because these false prophets will use Bible verses and speak the Christian language but lead people astray through false doctrine. These false prophets will teach the truth about the person and work of Jesus Christ, but their *soteriology,* or doctrine of salvation, will include water baptism. It will be difficult because the false teachers will have a correct understanding of the person and work of Jesus, but their soteriology will state that if you simply make a profession of faith, you're saved. These false prophets will completely ignore Jesus' hard sayings of counting the costs and submitting and trusting Christ (Luke 14:25–33). It will be difficult because the false prophets will give enough truth in their lie to make the lie believable. It will be difficult because these false prophets may purposefully be leading people astray. It will be difficult because some false prophets will not even know that they are false prophets and teachers. John says in 1 John 4:1, "Dear friends, do not believe every spirit, but test the spirits to see whether they are from God, because many false prophets have gone out into the world." John calls for the testing of the doctrine because many—*polus* meaning "much, many, high in number, multitudinous, great in amount"—false prophets have gone out into the world. It will be difficult because the only way to know if a false prophet is truly false is by becoming a good fruit examiner.

So what fruit is Jesus talking about? Jesus is talking about two fruits: examining the false prophet's doctrine and examining the false prophet's walk of life. Jesus is saying that you will need to pay attention to what the false teacher is teaching and discern if it lines up with God's Word. You will also need to pay attention to the fruit of their lives. John told his listeners to test the spirits to see if they were from God. The word *test* is translated from the original word *dokimazo*. *Dokimazo* means "to put to the test, prove, examine, to put to the test to reveal what is good." This word carries with it the sense of how they tested metals. They would test metals by heating up the element and burning away impurities to see what was pure versus what was counterfeit or fake. The Bereans were commended of this in Acts 17 where they would take Paul's message and examine the Scriptures every day to see if what Paul said was true (Acts 17:10–12). Comparing a false teacher's life and teaching against the Word of God is the only way to judge a teacher's fruit.

It's also important to note that the fruit may not be an immoral life and a false doctrine. No, what will make this difficult is that the false prophets may have a moral life, but false doctrine. In the time when Jesus was on the earth, the Pharisees were known to be very "moral and law abiding" people. However, they were outside God's kingdom. It may be easier to find a false prophet by their life, but it is much more difficult when the false prophet teaches truth, mixes in error, and lives a moral life. Jesus is saying that it will be difficult to find and enter the narrow gate because it will take searching the Scriptures and being knowledgeable in them to discern truth from error and will require being a good fruit inspector.

The True and False Disciples

Matthew 7:21–23—"Not everyone who says to Me, 'Lord, Lord,' will enter the kingdom of heaven, but the one who does the will of My Father who is in heaven will enter. Many will say to Me on that day, 'Lord, Lord, did we not prophesy in Your name, and in Your name cast out demons, and in Your name perform many miracles?' And then I will declare to them, 'I never knew you; leave Me, you who practice lawlessness.'"

Jesus goes on to clarify that it will be difficult to enter through the narrow gate because people will be self-deceived. More specifically, Jesus is talking about those who make verbal professions of faith, but never came to saving faith. In verse 21, Jesus says, "Not everyone who says to Me, 'Lord, Lord,' will enter the kingdom of heaven, but the one who does the will of My Father who is in heaven will enter." First, note the "Lord, Lord" statement. These are self-deceived people that knew who the Lord was. In fact, they said "Lord" twice, which indicates that they really believed that they were servants or followers of the Lord. Jesus is saying that you could spend your whole life in the church as a baptized and confirmed member, attend church every Sunday, be in good standing as a member, but not have saving faith.

Also note that Jesus says, "The one who does the will of My Father who is in heaven will enter." Likewise, in Matthew 12:48–50, Jesus says, "Who is my mother, and who are my brothers?" Pointing to his disciples, he said, "Here are my mother and my brothers. For whoever does the will of my Father in heaven is my brother and sister and mother." One must be careful to explain "doing the will of the Father." Jesus is ruling out salvation by works or salvation by faith plus works as He says in Matthew 5:48, "Be perfect, therefore, as your heavenly Father is perfect." No one can attain to this standard of perfection, and all fall short (Romans 3:10–20, 3:23). Jesus is not teaching salvation by works for this would completely contradict the doctrine of justification by faith. No, what Jesus is saying is that those who have been born from above, those who have repented, and those who have turned to Christ in saving faith will do the will of the Father. Jesus is saying there are self-deceived people that were never born again and never had the gift of faith and repentance, but were religious and were in the church.

Jesus goes on in verse 22 to say that *polus* or many will say to him on that day, "Lord, Lord did we not prophesy in your name and in your name drive out demons and in your name perform many miracles?" These people were so self-deceived. First, notice that Jesus says "many" will come to Him on either the Day of Judgment or Day of the Lord and believe that they were Christians. They will come to the Lord and say, "Lord, I taught Sunday School. Lord I was baptized. Lord I was confirmed. Lord I made a profession of faith. Lord I attended church every Sunday. Lord, I was an elder at the church. Lord, I started a ministry at the church. Lord, I taught adult Bible study. Lord, I gave offerings of 20% of my salary. Lord, I prayed every day. Lord, I read my Bible every day. Lord, I never committed adultery. Lord, I never had an abortion. Lord, I was never an immoral person. Lord, I lived a very good life." These people thought they had a connection to Jesus Christ which makes this completely devastating in the end.

Jesus says in the end, "Depart from me, you evildoers." What a shock. The most religious people, those who were outwardly moral, those who appeared the most religious, will get the most shocking and devastating news of their life. They will be told by the Lord that He never knew them. Jesus is not saying that He had no idea who they were for Christ is omniscient and knows all things. He has numbered the hairs on everyone's head (Matthew 10:30). What Jesus is saying is that He never knew them in a relational way. In fact, the word *know* is translated from the original word *ginóskó*. *Ginóskó* means "to come to know, recognize, perceive," but, properly, it means "to know through personal experience." For example, in Matthew 1:25, it says of Joseph as translated in the New King James Version, "and did not know her till she had brought forth her firstborn Son." In the original language it says, "*Kai ouk eginosken auten,*" which could also be translated, "And knew her not." The word *knew* is another form of the word *ginóskó*, which speaks of a knowing through deep personal experience. Jesus is saying He never knew these people in a personal or relational way. Sure, He knew of them and everything about them, but He didn't know them as His servants, brothers, sisters, friends, or coheirs. These are those who have not been regenerated by the Holy Spirit and have not been given the gift of repentance or faith. However, they were religious people that did religious things. Their end assessment on the last day will be one of utter devastation. Jesus could have also said it this way:

- Depart from me, you lawless, religious person, you never had a saving relationship with me.
- Depart from me, you whitewashed tomb, I never knew you as a child of God.
- Depart from me, you who are religious, you were never one of my sheep.

Two Ways to Listen

Matthew 7:24–27—"Therefore, everyone who hears these words of Mine, and acts on them, will be like a wise man who built his house on the rock. And the rain fell and the floods came, and the winds blew and slammed against that house; and yet it did not fall, for it had been founded on the rock. And everyone who hears these words of Mine, and does not act on them, will be like a foolish man who built his house on the sand. And the rain fell and the floods came, and the winds blew and slammed against that house; and it fell—and its collapse was great."

Let's recap quickly. Jesus is saying that the way to life through the narrow gate is going to be hard to find and it's going to be hard to enter (Matthew 7:13–14). Jesus is saying that there are going to be many false prophets that are going to make the narrow gate even more difficult to find and enter because of false teaching that leads people astray (Matthew 7:15–20). Jesus is saying that there are going to be a great multitude of people professing to be Christians but will be self-deceived and ultimately damned

(Matthew 7:21–23). Finally, Jesus ends His sermon with an ominous note. Jesus declares that there are two ways to receive His Word. He says that there are people who hear God's Word and put it into practice (v. 24–25) and there are those who hear His Word and do not put them into practice (v. 26–27). Much could be explained on just these three verses, but it's important to note the following about Christ's illustration here:

- Both builders built houses. (v. 24–27)
- One builder heard the Word and acted on it. (v. 24–25)
- One builder heard the Word and didn't act on it. (v. 26–27)
- The houses look alike, but the only difference is the foundation which no one can see. (v. 24–27)
- Both builders were in the same location, but one builder dug down deep and the other didn't. (Luke 6:48)
- Both houses underwent the same storm. (v. 24–27)
- The builder who heard Christ's Word and acted on them had a house that survived the storm. (v. 25)
- The builder who heard Christ's Word and did not act on them had a house that did not survive the storm. (v. 27)

Here Christ is calling for a decision. Either you will hear His Word and act upon it, or you will hear His Word and not act on it. Please note that you could hear His Word and agree with it, believe that it's correct, and believe that it's right, but never act on His words. In Luke 11:28, Jesus says, "On the contrary, blessed are those who hear the word of God and keep it." Jesus also says in John 10:27 of His sheep, "My sheep listen to my voice; I know them, and they follow me." James, the half-brother of Jesus, says in James 1:22, "But prove yourselves doers of the word, and not just hearers who deceive themselves." The Puritans used to call those who heard the Word and did nothing "practical atheists." Although they heard the Word, it made no impact to their life in such a way that would cause them to act upon it. Although they heard the Word, they never bore any fruit (Parable of the Soils). Let's also notice that the builder who heard the Word and acted upon it dug down deep (Luke 6:48). This was no quick decision. This was no emotional moment. No, this person heard the Word and performed soul searching examination with the Word of God. This person took the time to dig the hole and perform all necessary preparation of laying a proper foundation. As noted in Matthew 7:13–14, this is the person that searched for the gate, searched for the way to enter it, counted the costs, and entered through the gate by repentance and faith (Mark 1:15–16). Lastly, notice that although the two religious houses look the same, one ends in complete disaster. In fact, during the time of judgment, the builder realizes that the whole religious house that was built is destroyed. The builder's house which was destroyed will hear those terrible words, "Depart from me, you evildoer, I never knew you."

We should see Christ's seriousness on entering through the narrow gate and the dangers and difficulties with entering through it in Matthew 7:13–27:

- We are commanded to enter through the narrow gate. (Matthew 7:13)
- It is agonizing and a struggle to enter through the narrow gate. (Luke 13:22)
- There is only one narrow gate which is Jesus Christ. (John 10:7, 9)
- The gate is narrow and must be entered through in a specific way and on Jesus' terms. (Matthew 7:13–14)
- We must enter the gate urgently as many are already on the broad way and headed towards eternal hell. (Matthew 7:13)
- The gate that leads to destruction is wide and is full of false religions outside of Christianity as well as false gospels that are taught in Christianity. (Matthew 7:13)

- The broad road allows you to live your life any way you choose but, in the end, leads to destruction. (Matthew 7:13)
- Many or most of humanity enter through the broad gate and walk the broad road. (Matthew 7:13)
- The narrow way is tight, compressed, rubbed together, and is lived according to God's Word. (Matthew 7:14)
- There are few that find the narrow gate. (Matthew 7:14)
- Once you are justified, you will instantly be on the narrow road. (Matthew 7:14)
- The narrow gate will be hard to find because of false teachers and prophets. (Matthew 7:15)
- False prophets and teachers will be very deceptive and hard to identify. (Matthew 7:15)
- There will be many false teachers and prophets. (1 John 4:1)
- False prophets and teachers must be known by their fruit. (Matthew 7:16–20)
- False prophets and teachers can only be identified by the fruit of their doctrine or life. (Matthew 7:20)
- It will be hard to find the narrow gate because there will be many false disciples. (Matthew 7:21–23)
- False disciples will be self-deceived into believing they are true believers. (Matthew 7:21–22)
- False disciples will be involved in church life and religious activity. (Matthew 7:21–22)
- False disciples will be shocked on the Day of Judgment. (Matthew 7:23)
- It will be hard to enter through the narrow gate because we are easily self-deceived, and we must listen to God's Word and obey it. (Matthew 7:24–27)
- There is danger in someone who hears God's Word and agrees with it, but never acted on it. (Matthew 7:24–25)

- There is danger that one can be self-deceived into believing they are a Christian and find out, on the last day, that they were never a follower or believer in Christ. (Matthew 7:27)

As you can see, this world is a dangerous place and Jesus warned people to decide between eternal life and eternal hell. Let's consider these warnings of Jesus as we look into how Jesus called everyone to enter through the narrow gate.

CHAPTER 15

Entering the Narrow Gate through Saving Faith in Jesus Christ

Luke 14:25–33—Now large crowds were going along with Him; and He turned and said to them, "If anyone comes to Me, and does not hate his own father and mother and wife and children and brothers and sisters, yes, and even his own life, he cannot be my disciple. Whoever does not carry his own cross and come after Me cannot be my disciple. For which one of you, when he wants to build a tower, does not first sit down and calculate the cost to see if he has enough to complete it? Otherwise, when he was laid a foundation and is not able to finish, all who observe it begin to ridicule him, saying, 'This man began to build and was not able to finish.' Or what king, when he sets out to meet another king in battle, will not first sit down and consider whether he is strong enough with ten thousand men to encounter the one coming against him with twenty thousand? Or else, while the other is still far away, he sends a delegation and asks

> *for terms of peace. So then, none of you can be My disciple who does not give up all his possessions."*
>
> *Luke 9:23–24—Then he said to them all: "Whoever wants to be my disciple must deny themselves and take up their cross daily and follow me. For whoever wants to save their life will lose it, but whoever loses their life for me will save it."*

Jesus said some of the hardest words that have ever been spoken. His words can be comforting, full of grace, full of peace, full of mercy, full of love, and full of joy. However, Jesus' words can also be demanding, sharp, piercing, scary, towering, hard, and overwhelming. One of the most popular verses in the Bible is John 3:16, "For God so loved the world, that he gave His only begotten Son, that whoever believes in Him shall not perish, but have eternal life." And there are verses such as Matthew 7:13–14, Matthew 7:21–23, and Luke 13:22–30 where Jesus states that a large majority of mankind will perish and go to hell, and only a few will be saved. It's important to compare a verse like John 3:16 against a verse such as Luke 14:25–33, for in these Scriptures we see the evangelistic call of Jesus Christ where He invites all men to come to Him in saving faith. On the one hand, you can look at John 3:16 and say it's just having mental assent to the facts of the person and work of Jesus Christ. On the other hand, you can look at a verse like Luke 14:25–33 and say that Christ is calling someone to work for their salvation. Let's look at some examples of how Christ evangelistically called people to saving faith, which includes what people would call His "HARD" sayings as well as His "EASY" sayings:

EASY—John 3:16—For God so loved the world, that he gave his only begotten Son, that whoever believes in Him shall not perish, but have eternal life.

HARD—Luke 13:5—I tell you no, but unless you repent, you will all likewise perish.

- Note that in John 3:16 you will perish if you don't believe and in Luke 13:5 you will perish if you don't repent.

EASY—John 3:18—He who believes in Him is not judged; he who does not believe has been judged already, because he has not believed in the name of the only begotten Son of God.

HARD—Luke 13:3—I tell you, no, but unless you repent, you will all likewise perish.

- Note that in John 3:18 you will be judged or condemned if you do not believe in Jesus, and in Luke 13:3 you will perish if you don't repent

EASY—Romans 10:13—For "Everyone who calls on the name of the Lord will be saved."

HARD—Matthew 11:21–22— "Woe to you, Chorazin! Woe to you, Bethsaida! For if the miracles that were performed in you had been performed in Tyre and Sidon, they would have repented long ago in sackcloth and ashes. But I tell you it will be more bearable for Tyre and Sidon on the Day of Judgment than for you."

- Note that Romans 10:13 says that if you simply call on the name of the Lord you will be saved and in Matthew 10:21–22 Jesus calls damnation on two cities for their failure to repent.

EASY—John 3:36—He who believes in the Son has eternal life; but he who does not obey the Son will not see life, but the wrath of God abides on him.

HARD—Luke 24:47—And that repentance for forgiveness of sins would be proclaimed in His name to all the nations, beginning from Jerusalem.

- Note in John 3:36 that Jesus says if you believe in the Son you have eternal life and in Luke 24:47 that repentance for forgiveness of sins is what is proclaimed in Jesus' name.

EASY—John 7:38—He who believes in Me, as the Scripture said, from his innermost being will flow rivers of living water.

HARD—Acts 5:31—He is the one whom God exalted to His right hand as a Prince and a Savior, to grant repentance to Israel, and forgiveness of sins.

- Note in John 7:38 that Jesus says all who believe in Him will have the Holy Spirit (see John 7:39) and in Acts 5:31 it talks about Jesus granting repentance for the forgiveness of sins.

EASY—John 11:25–26—Jesus said to her, "I am the resurrection and the life; he who believes in Me will live even if he dies, and everyone who lives and believes in Me will never die. Do you believe this?"

HARD—Matthew 10:37–39—He who loves father or mother more than Me is not worthy of Me; and he who loves son or daughter more than Me is not worthy of Me. And he who does not take his cross and follow after Me is not worthy of Me. He who has found his life will lose it, and he who has lost his life for My sake will find it.

- Note that in John 11:25–26 it says that all who believe in Jesus will never die (i.e., have eternal life) and note in Matthew 10:37–39 Jesus lays down conditions on becoming a disciple and accepting Him as Lord and Savior.

EASY—John 6:47—Truly, truly, I say to you, he who believes has eternal life.

HARD—Luke 10:26–27— "If anyone comes to Me, and does not hate his own father and mother and wife and children and brothers and sisters, yes, and even his own life, he cannot be My disciple. Whoever does not carry his own cross and come after Me cannot be My disciple.

- Note that in John 6:47 it says if you believe you will have eternal life and in Luke 10:26–27 Jesus lays down conditions on becoming a disciple and accepting Him as Lord and Savior.

EASY—Acts 10:43—Of Him all the prophets bear witness that through His name everyone who believes in Him receives forgiveness of sins.

HARD—Mark 8:34–35—And he summoned the crowd with His disciples, and said to them, "If anyone wishes to come after Me, he must deny himself, and take up his cross and follow Me. For whoever wishes to save his life will lose it, but whoever loses his life for my sake and the gospel's will save it."

- Note that in Acts 10:43 it says that all who believe in Jesus will receive forgiveness of sins and in Mark 8:34–35 Jesus lays down conditions on becoming a disciple and accepting Him as Lord and Savior.

EASY—John 1:12—But as many as received Him, to them He gave the right to become children of God, even to those who believe in His name.

HARD—John 12:24–25—Truly, truly, I say to you, unless a grain of wheat falls into the earth and dies, it remains alone; but if it dies, it bears much fruit. He who loves his life loses it, and he who hates his life in this world will keep it to life eternal.

- Note that in John 1:12 it says that if you receive and believe in Jesus, you will be a child of God and in John 12:24–25 Jesus lays down conditions on accepting or receiving Him as Lord and Savior.

EASY—Romans 10:9—that if you confess with your mouth Jesus as Lord, and believe in your heart that God raised Him from the dead, you will be saved

HARD—Matthew 16:24–26—Then Jesus said to His disciples, "If anyone wishes to come after Me, he must deny himself, and take up his cross and follow Me. For whoever wishes to save his life will lose it; but whoever loses his life for My sake will find it. For what will it profit a man if he gains the whole world and forfeits his soul? Or what will a man give in exchange for his soul?"

- Note that in Romans 10:9 Paul says if you confess Jesus as Lord and believe in your heart that God raised Him from the dead, you will be saved and in Matthew 16:24–26 Jesus lays down conditions on becoming a disciple and accepting Him as Lord and Savior.

Looking at some of these verses regarding salvation can be difficult. On the one hand, Jesus talks about believing in Him for eternal Life. On the other hand, He talks about the need for repentance. Complicating it even further, He sets forth conditions on what it means to be His disciple or to come to saving faith.

It's very dangerous to take the "EASY" verses and ignore the "HARD" verses. What can end up happening is conjuring a false faith that teaches saving faith is just "believing" or agreeing to or having mental assent to gospel facts. However, if the "HARD" verses are not properly explained, it could seem like Jesus and the Scriptures are teaching works unto salvation or working for your salvation. It's vitally important to call people to faith in

Christ and the call should always be aligned with Scripture and consistent with what Christ called for.

Jesus' Call to Saving Faith

Luke 14:25–33—Now large crowds were going along with Him; and He turned and said to them, "If anyone comes to Me, and does not hate his own father and mother and wife and children and brothers and sisters, yes, and even his own life, he cannot be my disciple. Whoever does not carry his own cross and come after Me cannot be my disciple. For which one of you, when he wants to build a tower, does not first sit down and calculate the cost to see if he has enough to complete it? Otherwise, when he was laid a foundation and is not able to finish, all who observe it begin to ridicule him, saying, 'This man began to build and was not able to finish.' Or what king, when he sets out to meet another king in battle, will not first sit down and consider whether he is strong enough with ten thousand men to encounter the one coming against him with twenty thousand? Or else, while the other is still far away, he sends a delegation and asks for terms of peace. So then, none of you can be My disciple who does not give up all his possessions."

We've noted above that Jesus had some "easy" sayings regarding salvation, but then He also had some "hard" sayings regarding salvation. Jesus said that anyone who believes in Him will be saved as in John 3:16. Also, He laid out the cost of discipleship required to follow Him which was extremely high. This section is going to explain Jesus' call to entering the narrow gate through saving faith.

Luke 14:25—now large crowds were going along with Him, and He turned and said to them

Throughout Jesus' ministry He had large crowds following Him. Some of them followed Him because they were interested in His teaching, some people followed Him because they wanted to be fed (John 6:26), some followed Him because they thought He was a prophet or John the Baptist (Matthew 16:13–16), some followed Him because of the signs He performed by healing others (John 6:2), some followed Him because they were true disciples and believed He was the Messiah (Mark 8:29), and many people followed Him for several other reasons. Jesus turned to them and gave them His conditions for entrance into the kingdom. It's as if Jesus saw that the crowds were getting too large, and He wanted to let them know of the cost of becoming His disciple.

Jesus never hid His cost of discipleship and the demand that was required to follow Him. Jesus never hid His call of believing in Him in the fine print. His call to being a disciple was always front-loaded in His messages. In fact, Jesus was never seeking to make following Him easy. If you look at Jesus' call to discipleship, you could never accuse Him of trying to build a large crowd with His message or terms of entering the kingdom. Jesus calls for crossbearers and not merely crosswearers. We will either be abandoned to Christ or abandoned by Christ. We cannot have Christ on our own terms. There is no crown without first bearing a cross. There is no religion without repentance. There is no blessedness without brokenness. There is no salvation without sacrifice. There is no church without commitment. There is no heaven without holiness. Jesus will now turn to the large crowd and set forth His terms of discipleship, or rather, entrance into the kingdom of God. Pay attention, this is His call on entering the narrow gate. The One who issues the call sets the terms.

Luke 14:26—"If anyone comes to Me and does not hate his own father, mother, wife, children, brothers, sisters, yes, and even his own life, he cannot be my disciple."

Jesus starts by evangelistically inviting all people to come to Him. Just as He said in John 7:37, "On the last and greatest day of the feast, Jesus stood and cried out, saying, 'If anyone is thirsty, let him come to me and drink.'" Jesus, the narrow gate, is explaining how to enter through the narrow gate. However, everyone is required to enter through the narrow gate on Jesus' terms. It's important to notice the word *disciple. Disciple* is translated from the word *mathētés. Mathētés* means "a learner, a disciple, and pupil." Properly, this is a learner or follower of Christ who learns the doctrines of Scripture and the lifestyle required to follow Christ. Jesus is saying that if you want to be a follower, a believer, or a disciple of His, then here are the terms of entering the kingdom through the narrow gate.

First, Jesus is going to start with relationships and lay down His terms and conditions for entering the narrow gate. Jesus' words would certainly shock people when He said, "If anyone comes to Me and does not hate his own father, mother, wife, children, brothers, and yes, even his own life, he cannot be My disciple." Let's note that Jesus is not calling for His disciples to hate anyone. In Matthew 10:37, Jesus says, "The one who loves father or mother more than Me is not worthy of Me; and the one who loves son or daughter more than Me is not worthy of Me." In Matthew 5:43, Jesus says, "You have heard that it was said, 'Love your neighbor and hate your enemy.' But I tell you, love your enemies and pray for those who persecute you, that you may be children of Your Father in heaven. He causes his sun to rise on the evil and the good, and sends rain on the righteous and the unrighteous." God also says in the Fourth Commandment to, "Honor your father and your mother." Additionally, Jesus, when being tested, states in Matthew 22:39 that the second greatest commandment is "Love your neighbor as yourself." Jesus is not calling for hate. He commands that we love our enemies, love our neighbor as ourselves, and honor our father and mother. What Jesus is doing is showing contrast or preference. He uses this same method of showing preference in Matthew 6:24, where He says, "No one can serve two masters. Either you will hate one and love the other, or you will be devoted to the one and despise the other. You cannot serve both God and money." As in

Jesus' example of serving both God and money, Jesus is simply saying that both God and money cannot have the same top priority as you will ultimately love one more than the other. Jesus is purposefully creating extremes. He is pitting one's affections of one's most loved ones against one's affections to Himself. Jesus is saying is that if you want to be His disciple then your affections for Him must be far greater than the love for those in your closest concentric circle.

Jesus starts with the people that mean most to you. Jesus starts with your father, mother, wife, and children. **Christ is calling for your total allegiance and affection. Your allegiance and affections towards Him must be far greater than the affections and allegiance you have with the people that are most important to you.** Jesus makes a shocking statement at the end of this verse. Jesus says, *"ou dynatai einai mou mathetes" Dynatei* means "to be able" or "to have power." *Ou* means "no" or "not." *Einai* means "to be." *Mou* is a personal pronoun and means "I." *Mathetes* is a disciple or learner, but specifically, a follower or learner of Christ. So, let's put this statement together and understand what Jesus is saying in a few different ways:

- If anyone comes to Me and has greater affections for his father, mother, wife, children, or brothers and sisters, he is not able to be My disciple.
- If anyone comes to Me and sees his father, mother, wife, children, or brothers as more important than Me, he has no ability to be My disciple.
- If anyone comes to Me and finds any relationship more important than their relationship with Me, they are not one of My disciples.
- If anyone comes to Me and has a relationship or allegiance to anyone that is more important to them than Me, you are not in My kingdom.

It's also important to note here that Jesus is not saying, you may be able to be My disciple. No, He is stating that you cannot be His disciple. *May* is a word of permission. *Cannot* is a word of ability. Jesus is requiring absolute allegiance and affection over every relationship you have on this earth. When it comes down to listening to your mother and father or listening to Jesus, which one will it be? Do you have more affections and allegiance to your wife or Jesus? Jesus is asking whether you've done your searching and seeking and found Him to be of greater importance than your closest relationship. If not, you're simply not a disciple of His and you've made an eternally fatal assessment.

Note that in Matthew 10:37, instead of *hate* He says, *worthy*. As we learned earlier, *axios* can also mean "worthy, worthy of, deserving, or suitable." Another way of describing this word is to weigh in, assigning the matching value or worth-to-worth (i.e., as the assessment in keeping with how something "weighs in" on God's balance scale of truth). Jesus says that if you love anyone in this world more than Him, you're simply just not worthy to be His disciple.

Jesus really starts intensifying His call as He lays down another term of becoming His disciple. He says that we must hate our own life. Jesus demands that you evaluate your own life and determine whether submitting and committing your life to Him is more valuable than keeping it. Jesus was never shy about calling people to evaluate their lives and asking them to determine if their current relationships, personal interests, personal hobbies, personal sins, or personal belongings were more important than Him. To further clarify Jesus' call of hating one's own life, we can look to other portions of Scripture to understand this call of "hating yourself" as He is not advocating suicide, self-mutilation, or anything of this nature.

Jesus' calls to discipleship or saving faith often included a command to deny yourself which could also be understood as "hating your own life" as noted in Luke 14:26. Denying yourself and hating yourself have the same connotation. In Luke 9:23, Jesus says, "Whoever wants to be my disciple must deny themselves and take up their cross daily and follow me. For whoever wants to save their life will lose it, but whoever loses their life for me will save it." In Matthew 16:24, Jesus says, "Whoever wants to be my disciple must deny themselves and take up their cross and follow me. For whoever wants to save their life will lose it, but whoever loses their life for me will find it." In Mark 8:34–35, Jesus says, "Whoever wants to be my disciple must deny themselves and take up their cross and follow me. For whoever wants to save their life will lose it, but whoever loses their life for me and for the gospel will save it." In Matthew 10:39, Jesus says, "Whoever finds their life will lose it, and whoever loses their life for my sake will find it." In John 12:25, Jesus says, "Anyone who loves their life will lose it, while anyone who hates their life in this world will keep it for eternal life." Jesus said several times that one must *"deny themselves."* This word is very strong and in the original language is *aparneomai. Aparneomai* means "to deny, disown, repudiate, forsake, or reject." This same word is used when Peter denied Jesus three times. Just as Peter said, "I don't know the man," so Jesus calls us to say the same thing to our lives which is to say to ourselves, "I don't know the man. I'm sold out, submitted, and committed to Jesus." **When Jesus is telling you to deny yourself or hate yourself, He is saying that you must repent of your sins, say goodbye to your worldly desires and pride, and say goodbye to self-will in exchange for His yoke, His will, and His rule over your life**. In other words, Jesus is calling men everywhere to look at their sin, look at their life, and make a judgment call. Is Jesus Christ important enough to submit, commit, and entrust your life to? If not, then *"ou dynatai einai mou mathetes"* or "You cannot be my disciple."

Let's notice that Jesus is giving a call to get to know Him. A faithful gospel call will include the person of Jesus, the work of Jesus, and then the evangelistic call to faith in Him. Jesus is inviting us to get to know Him. Just like when you are dating and getting to know someone in the hope of making the final decision to get married, so a similar analogy could be made here. Jesus is inviting you to see His person, which includes being the second person of the Godhead, the Son of God, the Christ, or the Messiah who was promised in the Old Testament. Jesus is true God and true man. Jesus was born of a virgin. Jesus is the Great I AM, the judge, the only savior, and more. Jesus is inviting you to see His work which includes His sinless life, His miracles which attest to His deity and Messiahship, His death on the cross for the sins of His people, and His imputed righteousness that He gives to all those who come to Him in saving faith. He is inviting you to see His resurrection which confirms His victory over all powers. He is inviting you to view His ascension into heaven and His current enthronement at the right hand of God. He is inviting you to see His High Priestly work in heaven, the guarantee of eternal life for all that come to Him, and more. Jesus is not calling us to decide without getting to know Him or His work. Just as we would take time to get to know someone before we decide to marry that person, so Jesus invites us to get to know Him. Jesus is inviting us to learn about Him and seek Him through the Scriptures. This is no blind date. This is no quick commitment. Jesus gives the invitation to know His person and work and then commands and demands an answer.

Let's notice that if you have come to Jesus and conclude that the created things in your life are more important than the creator, than you have made a disastrous assessment or judgment. If you don't see the weight of your sins and condemnation as a big deal, then Christ is not a big deal to you. If you have not seen your personal sin as the priority that needs to be immediately and urgently addressed, then Christ has no meaning to you.

- Man calls sin an accident. God calls sin an abomination.
- Man calls sin a blunder. God calls sin blasphemy.

- Man calls sin an error. God calls sin enmity.
- Man calls sin a fascination. God calls sin a fatality.
- Man calls sin an infirmity. God calls sin iniquity.
- Man calls sin a trifle. God calls sin a transgression.
- Man calls sin a mistake. God calls sin madness.
- Man calls sin weakness. God calls sin wickedness.
- Man calls sin an oops. God calls sin an offense.

Let's also notice that the attitude when coming to Jesus is incredibly important. Jesus describes the person who has come to the end of themselves and have seen their sins as great and seen Christ as greater. Jesus talks about this person in the Beatitudes in Matthew 5:3–6. We spoke earlier how Matthew 5:3–6 describes repentance and turning to God! Jesus starts out in verse 3 where He says, "Blessed are the poor in spirit, for theirs is the kingdom of heaven." *Blessed* here refers to "those who have divine favor with God." The original word *makarios* is translated to "blessed" in the English language. *Makarios* means "blessed or happy." The reason these individuals are happy or blessed is because they have divine favor or God's grace. Here is how you can think about this attitude which marks those who enter the kingdom of God. These first four Beatitudes mark the attitudes of those who enter through the narrow gate and the attitudes that characterize the Christian walk of life.

- Matthew 5:3—Blessed are the poor in spirit, for theirs is the kingdom of heaven.
    - *Ptóchos* has been translated to "poor" but it means beggarly poor of one who crouches and cowers because all he can do is to hold out his hand. It is the extreme opposite of rich. In other words, Jesus is saying, blessed are those who are so spiritually bankrupt in their spirit and realize they have no right to stand before God. Blessed are those who are so troubled and anguished

in their spirit that all they can do is crouch and ask for mercy from God. These people are blessed for theirs is the kingdom of God. Isaiah 57:15 is another excellent cross-reference on poor in spirit where the LORD says, "I live in a high and holy place, but also with the one who is contrite and lowly in spirit, to revive the spirit of the lowly and to revive the heart of the contrite." Isaiah 66:2 is an excellent cross-reference that talks about the poor in spirit where the LORD says, "These are the ones I look on with favor: those who are humble and contrite in spirit, and who tremble at my word."

- Matthew 5:4 – Blessed are those who mourn, for they will be comforted.
    - *Pentheó* has been translated "mourn" and it means mourning as if grieving over a death. This mourning is so severe that it takes possession of a person and cannot be hidden. This is not talking about those who mourn over losing a job or a loved one. It cannot mean that because even people in false religions mourn over such things. No, Jesus is saying that those who mourn, weep, and wail over their own personal sins against God have divine favor. Those who will mourn over how they have sinned against God will be comforted. Those who will say the same thing about their sin as what God says about sin, will be comforted by God. Joel 2:12–13 is an excellent cross-reference for mourning over sin, "'Even now,' declares the LORD, 'return to me with all your heart, with fasting and weeping and mourning.' Rend your heart and not your garments. Return to the LORD your GOD, for he is gracious and compassionate, slow to anger and abounding in love, and he relents from sending calamity."
- Matthew 5:5—Blessed are the meek for they shall inherit the earth.

  - First, the word *meekness* does not mean weakness. No, this word carries with it the idea of submission unto a master. It could also be thought of as strength under control. This is a person who will no longer exercise untamed power and control but will submit to a master. This word was used to describe breaking in a horse. Before breaking in a horse, the horse would buck, bite, and kick, but after the horse had been broken in and the bit and bridle put into its mouth, it would be considered "meeked." This is not to say the horse lost its power, but rather, the power remained and was directed by its master. So it is with those who enter the kingdom. They come in submission to God. They are meeked because of their sin and submit to the Lord Jesus Christ. Those who are meek shall inherit the earth. Those who are meek because of their sin and submit to the authority of Jesus Christ shall inherit "a new heaven and a new earth" (Revelation 21:1).
- Matthew 5:6—Blessed are those who hunger and thirst for righteousness, for they will be satisfied.
  - Thinking of hunger and thirsting is hard in the United States or in First World countries. Most people have never experienced this in their lives. However, for those who have been so hungry where they have no strength, have body aches, and body pains, they would know what this means. Likewise, those who are so deprived of water where they have dryness of throat, where they have no strength, and where they experience dehydration would know of this thirsting. Jesus is saying those who hunger and thirst for righteousness in such a way have divine favor from God. In other words, those who hunger and thirst for the righteousness that can only be found in Jesus Christ will be satisfied. Not only will they hunger and thirst for the righteousness of Christ

> for their justification before God, they will also be hungering and thirsting for more righteousness to be conformed to the image of the Son of God.

Matthew 5:3–6 is one of the clearest descriptions of true repentance where the sinner is intellectually aware of their personal spiritual bankruptcy before God (Matthew 5:3), they mourn over their sin against God and have Godly sorrow (Matthew 5:4, 2 Corinthians 7:10), they are meek and submissive under the Lord (Matthew 5:5), and they turn to Jesus for the righteousness they do not possess (Matthew 5:6). This is the person who has come to the end of themselves, and this is their attitude when entering through the narrow gate. These people have submitted and committed everything to Christ. They deny themselves. They are broken over sin. They long for Jesus and the righteousness He provides. This is the tax collector in Jesus' parable in Luke 18, where the tax collector stood at a distance and would not even look up to heaven, but said, "God have mercy on me the sinner." This is the person that cowers to God in spirit and only asks for mercy and never for justice. This is the attitude of repentance, self-denial, and self-hate that Christ is calling for. Jesus is calling for a radical repentance and allegiance to Him, but as He moves on, His cost and terms of becoming a disciple become even more demanding.

Luke 14:27—Whoever does not carry his own cross and come after Me cannot be My disciple.

Crucifixion was considered one of the most brutal and shameful modes of death. It likely had origins with the Assyrians and Babylonians and was eventually introduced to Rome by the Phoenicians in the third century BC. The Romans perfected crucifixion for five hundred years until it was abolished by Constantine I in the fourth century AD. Death could take from six hours to several days and could be due to aftereffects of compulsory scourging, maiming, hemorrhage, and dehydration causing hypovolemic shock. Death could also be precipitated by cardiac arrest. The attending Roman guards only left the site after the victim had died and would either break the victim's legs, stab the heart or chest with spears, or build a fire at the foot of the cross to asphyxiate the victim. Those who were crucified included slaves, disgraced soldiers, Christians, foreigners, and very rarely Roman citizens. The Jews knew what Jesus was talking about when Jesus said, "Whoever does not carry his own cross and come after Me cannot be my disciple." They had seen crucifixion before. They knew it was the death of deaths. They knew the cross meant agony. They knew the cross meant suffering. They knew the cross meant torture. They knew the cross meant shame. They knew the cross meant certain death.

Jesus' invitation to carry one's cross is an invitation to not only deny yourself, but to die to yourself. This is a death to self-will. This is a death to personal sins. This is a death to the lust of the flesh, the lust of the eyes, and the pride of life. This is not perfection, but it is the call to daily die to yourself. In fact, in Luke 9:23, Jesus says, "Whoever wants to be my disciple must deny themselves and take up their cross and follow me daily." This is an ongoing death to self. This is a daily death to self. Not only is this an open invitation, it's also a command. Notice that He invites everyone, but He still requires all His disciples to bear a cross and to do it daily.

Are you willing to so identify with Christ through faith that it costs you everything? Is following Christ worth losing your relationships, your personal interests, your belongings? Will you give up everything to gain Christ like Paul did (Philippians 3:4–9)? Is picking up your cross and identifying with Jesus worth the agony, worth the persecution, worth the shame, worth death? Christ may not require that you sell your house, sell your car, give up your job, but if that is in His plan, are you willing to pay the price? Is Christ worth this cost? Make a careful assessment.

Notice that He once again says, *"ou dynatai einai mou mathetes"* Whoever does not carry his own cross and come after Christ "cannot be His disciple." These are absolute terms. There is no negotiating with the gatekeeper. These are the terms of entrance into the kingdom. If entrance into the kingdom is just "believing" or "mental assent" to facts, then Jesus is a liar. Jesus is stating His terms of entrance through the narrow gate. Jesus is defining the call to saving faith. Christ called men to follow Him under these terms. Christ laid down the terms and conditions for entrance into His kingdom. His disciples must do the same as well.

Jesus also gives two parables in Matthew 13:44–46, those of the Hidden Treasure and the Pearl. In Matthew 13:44, He says, "The kingdom of heaven is like treasure hidden in a field. When a man found it, he hid it again, and then in his joy went and sold all he had and bought the field." This is speaking of a man who finds Jesus Christ, the forgiveness of sins, and eternal life. The man is filled with joy inexpressible and sells everything to buy the field. This more specifically talks about the joy and price people are willing to pay to enter the kingdom of God. This is the most valuable possession in the world that is worth the cost of a personal cross, denying yourself, repenting of sins, and submitting and trusting in Christ.

In Matthew 13:45–46 Jesus says, "Again, the kingdom of heaven is like a merchant looking for fine pearls. When he found one of great value, he went away and sold everything he had and bought it." There are differences in each parable, but the underlying theme is that those who have found the forgiveness of sins, Jesus Christ, and eternal life will pay the price because what they have found is so much more valuable than anything else in this life. This is the cross-carrying, self-denying, repentant faith that Jesus is calling for. Jesus is describing the sinner who is destitute, who finds the Savior, and loses their life to gain Him.

A book that would be of great value to Christians would be *Foxe's Book of Martyrs,* where it describes the killing of Christians from the apostolic age through the 1800s. You can see very clearly in the early church and throughout the church era that the disciples of Christ knew the terms of discipleship and the cost of following Christ:

- Stephen preached the gospel to the Jewish religious leaders and was stoned.
- About two thousand Christians, with Nicanor, one of the seven deacons along with Stephen, suffered martyrdom during the "persecution that arose about Stephen."
- James, the brother of John, was beheaded.
- Philip the Apostle was scourged, thrown into prison, and afterwards crucified.
- Matthew the Apostle was killed with a halberd in the city of Nadabah.
- Matthias, who was chosen to replace Judas, was stoned and then beheaded.
- Andrew the Apostle was crucified.
- John Mark was dragged to pieces by the people of Alexandria.
- Peter was crucified upside down.
- Paul gave his neck to the sword.
- Jude, the brother of James, was crucified.
- Bartholomew was cruelly beaten and then crucified by impatient idolaters.
- The apostle Thomas was run through with a spear.
- Luke was thought to have been hanged on an olive tree by the idolatrous priests of Greece.
- Nero, the sixth emperor of Rome, had Christians sewed up in skins of wild beasts and then attacked by dogs until they expired.
- Nero, the sixth emperor of Rome, dressed Christians in shirts made with wax, fixed to axletrees, and set them on fire in his gardens to illuminate them.

- Timothy severely reproved pagans, who celebrated a feast called Catagogion, and was beaten with them by their clubs and died two days later.
- Under Marcus Aurelius in AD 161, Marcus had some of the martyrs pass, with their already wounded feet, over thorns, nails, sharp shells, etc. Others were scourged until their sinews and veins lay bare and, after suffering the most excruciating tortures that could be devised, they were destroyed by the most terrible deaths.
- Polycarp, the bishop of Smyrna, was burned to death in the marketplace. The proconsul urged him saying, "Swear, and I will release thee; reproach Christ." Polycarp answered, "Eighty and six years have I served him, and he never once wronged me; how then shall I blaspheme my King, who hath saved me?"
- Eulalia, a Spanish lady of a Christian family, was known in her youth for sweetness of temper and solidity of understanding that was seldom found in women of her own age. She was apprehended by the magistrate in an attempt to convert her to paganism. However, she ridiculed the pagan deities with such harshness that the judge ordered her to be tortured. Her sides were accordingly torn by hooks, and her breasts burnt in the most shocking manner, until she died in the flames in AD 304.
- Valerius the bishop and Vincent the deacon were seized by the governor of Terragona. Vincent and Valerius were firm in their resolution for Christ. Valerius was banished and Vincent was racked. Vincent's limbs were dislocated, his flesh torn with hooks, and he was laid on a gridiron that was heated with fire underneath and spikes at the top which ran into his flesh. These torments did not change his resolution. He was sent to prison and confined in a dark dungeon strewn with sharp flints and pieces of

broken glass where he died on January 22, 304. His body was thrown into a river.

- Julitta, a Lycaonian of royal descent, was more celebrated for her virtues than noble blood. While on the rack, her child was killed before her face. Julitta of Cappadocia was a lady of distinguished capacity, great virtue, and uncommon courage. To complete the execution, Julitta had boiling pitch poured on her feet, her sides torn with hooks, and she received the conclusion of her martyrdom by being beheaded on April 16, 305.
- From the Revocation of the Edict of Nantes, which was an anti-Reformation policy by King Louis XIV, those who refused to hear Mass were sentenced to bastinado. The victims were held in place so that they could not move. During this time, the executioner would cruelly beat the victim with a rough cudgel or a knotty rope's end until the skin is flayed off his bones and he is near to death. They would apply a most tormenting mixture of vinegar and salt and consign him to an intolerable hospital where they would die.

This has always been the call to saving faith and following Christ. It is to repent from your sins, deny yourself, pick up your cross, submit your life to Christ, and trust in Christ as Lord and Savior for salvation. Additionally, Jesus says that this will be your daily way of life if you follow Him (Luke 9:23). Jesus says that anything short of this is not saving faith and you are not a disciple if you don't come to Him on His terms.

Luke 14:28–30—For which one of you, when he wants to build a tower, does not first sit down and calculate the cost, to see if he has enough to complete it? Otherwise, when he has laid a foundation and is not able to finish, all who are watching it will begin to ridicule him, saying, "This person began to build and was not able to finish!"

Jesus here is calling people to count the cost to follow Him. He has laid down His terms for being His disciple. He is asking everyone to stop and consider the cost. He does not want a quick decision. He does not want to coerce anyone. He is not guaranteeing what will happen in the next five, ten, or twenty years. He is simply stating that you will need to carefully consider whether you're willing to commit to Him. In an ultimate shame and honor society such as the Jewish culture, they would have understood this parable. They would know that it would be foolish to start to build a building without first determining whether they could finish. The one who had not carefully counted the costs and decided to build without considering the costs, would ultimately lead to great shame. Is it worth losing your life to gain Jesus? Christ is calling everyone to consider the cost of following Him as it requires a death to oneself and a submission and trust in Him.

Luke 14:31–32—Or what king, when he sets out to meet another king in battle, will not first sit down and consider whether he is strong enough with ten thousand men to face the one coming against him with twenty thousand? Otherwise, while the other is still far away, he sends a delegation and requests terms of peace.

The King will return one day, and He will not be coming as the suffering servant, but as the conquering King. This King will come to judge and wage war (Revelation 19:11). This King will come with His armies (Revelation 19:14). This King will strike down nations with His Word (Revelation 19:15). This King will tread upon His enemies with the wrath of God (Revelation 19:15). This King will kill and destroy His enemies (Revelation 19:21). This King will come with a wrath so horrible that people will cry for mountains and rocks to fall on them rather than suffer the wrath of the Lamb (Revelation 6:16–17). This is the King that is coming, and He has made terms of peace. Christ's terms of peace are stated in Luke 14:26–27 and further clarified in Matthew 5:3–6, 10:37–39, 13:44–46, 16:24–26; Mark 8:34–35; Luke 9:23–26, 18:9–14; and, John 12:24–26. He is coming against His enemies with strength and force. There is still time for the sinful man to come to terms of peace with this King. He has offered His terms of peace. This includes repentance, submission of your life, and trust in Him alone. Faith alone in Him justifies, but the gospel presentation is not complete without talking about the response of repentance and submission to Christ.

Luke 14:33—So then, none of you can be My disciple who does not give up all his own possessions.

Jesus has addressed relationships in verse 26. He has addressed crossbearing, self-denial, submission, and trust in verse 27. He has addressed the need for careful consideration in verses 28–30. He has addressed making the decision to come to terms of peace with God in verses 31–32. Jesus is now talking about possessions. As mentioned above, He may not ask you to give up everything, but you must be willing to give up everything if He calls you. In fact, in this life He may give you an abundance or more than you need. However, He may require everything of you. Regardless of what He decides, are you willing to give up everything for Him? Repentance is a gift (Acts 5:31, 11:18; 2 Timothy 2:25). Faith is a gift (Ephesians 2:8–9, Romans 5:15). Who could possibly respond to Christ's call to discipleship? Who can possibly respond in faith? Who can possibly be saved? Someone asked Jesus in Luke 13:23, "Lord, are only a few people going to be saved?" This is an extreme call to faith. How can it be that anyone would come to Christ on these terms of discipleship? The answer can be found in John 3:3, "Jesus responded and said to him, "Truly, truly, I say to you, unless someone is born from above he cannot see the kingdom of God." Only those born from above can respond to this call to discipleship in repentance and faith. Paul gives an account of his conversion to Christ. He starts by giving an account of his BC days or "Before Christ" days where he recalls in Philippians 3:4–6:

"Though I myself have reason for confidence in the flesh also. If anyone else thinks he has reason for confidence in the flesh, I have more: circumcised on the eighth day, of the people of Israel, of the tribe of Benjamin, a Hebrew of Hebrews; as to the law, a Pharisee; as to zeal, a persecutor of the church; as to righteousness under the law, blameless."

As you can see, before his conversion, Paul was an outwardly moral Pharisee, had great zeal for God's word, and was externally blameless. However, Paul transitions from his "Before Christ" days to his conversion in verses 7–9:

"But whatever gain I had, I counted as loss for the sake of Christ. Indeed, **I count everything as loss** because of the surpassing worth of knowing Christ Jesus my Lord. For his sake **I have suffered the loss of all things and count them as rubbish, in order that I may gain Christ and be found in him, not having a righteousness of my own that comes from the law, but that which comes through faith in Christ, the righteousness from God that depends on faith.**"

The apostle Paul, who taught the great doctrine of justification by faith, goes on to describe the call of saving faith in Philippians 3. Here, Paul looks at his religious rituals and ceremonies. Paul looks at his national heritage. Paul looks at his family relations. Paul looks at his external righteousness. Paul looks at all of this and counts it all as rubbish or *skybala* in the original language, which can refer to "refuse or dung." Paul did his accounting. Paul saw his liabilities and his assets. Paul put all his religious rituals, rites, and accomplishments on one side and Jesus Christ on the other side and found Christ was everything and everything else was dung. Christ's call to saving faith was the same call that Paul answered. Paul evaluated everything in his life and gave it up for Christ. The same apostle who wrote thirteen books of the New Testament and explained the doctrine of justification by faith is the same apostle who knew the call to saving faith and surely proclaimed this same call to saving faith in Christ.

When looking at verses such as John 3:16, John 3:36, Romans 10:13, Romans 10:9, and other verses which talk about believing and calling on the name of the Lord, one must also take a careful look at other portions of Scripture where Jesus is very specific on His terms of entrance through the narrow gate and into the kingdom of God. The call to saving faith can be found in verses such as Matthew 5:3–6, 10:37–39, 13:44–46; Mark 8:34–35; Luke 9:23–26, 14:25–33, 18:9–14; and, John 12:24–26. Luke 14:25–33 is one of the greatest gifts and passages in Scripture to help us understand Jesus' call to saving faith. When looking at the "easier" salvation Scriptures, it's very easy to come up with a doctrine of justification by believing or "mental assent" to Jesus and the gospel. However, if you just look at the "harder" verses, it's very easy to mistakenly preach a "works gospel." Both the "easier" and "harder" portions of Scripture must be used together to understand the call to saving faith. Stressing the intellectual, emotional, and volitional element of saving faith is vitally important just as much as teaching that faith and repentance are gifts that God gives. Luke 14:25–33 helps us understand the Lord's conditions to entering the narrow gate, becoming a disciple of Christ, or believing. Thus, saving faith and entering the narrow gate could be expressed as follows: ***Saving faith*** **is a gift from God where a sinner has knowledge of Jesus' person and work where a sinner will respond to Christ's person and work by denying themselves, picking up their cross, submitting and committing their life to Jesus, and trusting in Him only for salvation.**

Jesus is the friend of sinners. Jesus calls all men to Himself as in Matthew 11:28–30, "Come to me, all who are weary and burdened, and I will give you rest. Take my yoke upon you and learn from me, for I am gentle and humble in heart, and you will find rest for your souls. For my yoke is easy, and my burden is light." Jesus again affirms in John 6:37 that He will accept and save sinners where He says, "All those the Father gives me will come to me, and whoever comes to me I will never drive away." Jesus calls all men unto Himself. The call to salvation is open to everyone regardless of age, income, gender, nationality, ethnicity, and more. However, let us note that when we come to Jesus, Jesus has set forth the cost and terms of entrance into His kingdom.

So let's put this all together. In John 3:3 Jesus told Nicodemus, "Truly, truly, I say to you, unless someone is born again he cannot see the kingdom of God." We gave a definition of *regeneration,* or being born from above, which is: ***Regeneration* is the sovereign monergistic work of God the Holy Spirit in giving spiritual life to spiritually dead and sinful man so that man is enabled to repent and respond in saving faith to Jesus Christ.** In Mark 1:15, Jesus says, "The kingdom of God has come near. Repent and believe the good news!" Thus, given our definitions of *repentance* and *saving faith*, here is how Christ calls all men to enter through the narrow gate: ***Repentance* is a gift from God where the sinner understands his sin against God (intellect), has Godly sorrow and mourns over his sin against God (emotions and affections), and turns away from his sin and towards God for righteousness (will or volition). *Saving faith* is a gift from God where a sinner has knowledge of Jesus' person and work where a sinner will respond to Christ's person and work by denying themselves, picking up their cross, submitting and committing their life to Jesus and trusting in Him only for salvation.** Although there is much that could be discussed on the doctrine of assurance of salvation, such as the book of first John, evidence of entering through the narrow gate and being in union with Christ will be a lifelong walk of bearing fruits of repentance and saving faith. As Paul says in Colossians 2:6, "So then, just as you received Christ Jesus as Lord, continue to live your lives in him."

Martin Luther was certainly capable of talking about saving faith in such as a way as Christ where he says in an excerpt:

"Faith is not what some people think it is. Their human dream is a delusion. Because they observe that faith is not followed by good works or a better life, they fall into error, even though they speak and hear much about faith. 'Faith is not enough,' they say, 'You must do good works, you must be pious to be saved.' They think that, when you hear the gospel, you start working, creating by your own strength a thankful heart which says, 'I believe.' That is what they think true faith is. But, because this is a human idea, a dream, the heart never learns anything from it, so it does nothing and reform doesn't come for this 'faith,' either.

"Instead, *faith* is God's work in us that changes us and gives new birth from God (John 1:13). It kills the old Adam and makes us completely different people. It changes our hearts, our spirits, our thoughts, and all our powers. It brings the Holy Spirit with it. Yes, it is a living, creative, active, and powerful thing, this faith. Faith cannot help doing good works constantly. It doesn't stop to ask if good works ought to be done, but before anyone asks, it already has done them and continues to do them without ceasing. Anyone who does not do good works in this manner is an unbeliever. He stumbles around and looks for faith and good works, even though he does not know what faith or good works are. Yet he gossips and chatters about faith and good works with many words.

"*Faith* is a living, bold trust in God's grace, so certain of God's favor that it would risk death a thousand times trusting in it. Such a confidence and knowledge of God's grace makes you happy, joyful, and bold in your relationship to God and all creatures. The Holy Spirit makes this happen through faith. Because of it, you freely, willingly, and joyfully do good to everyone, serve everyone, suffer all kinds of things, love, and praise the God who has shown you such grace. Thus, it is just as impossible to separate faith and works as it is to separate heat and light from fire! Therefore, watch out for your own false ideas and guard against good-for-nothing gossips, who think they're smart enough to define faith and works, but really are the greatest of fools. Ask God to work faith in you, or you will remain forever without faith, no matter what you wish, say, or can do." (3)

We'll end with a story.

A pastor was giving a sermon on John 3:16 and Romans 3:23–28 to a young man. The pastor said, "If you would just believe in Jesus Christ as your savior, you will have eternal life and you have been justified by faith." There was a young man who was excited and talked to the pastor after the service in the narthex and said, "I believe in Jesus as the Son of God and my Savior and I've been justified by faith. I'm going to heaven!" The pastor said, "That is terrific young man! I'm so excited for you!" The young man then told the pastor, "I'm going to go home and tell my girlfriend of this great news." The pastor then said, "Oh, are you two living together?" The young man said, "Yes, we've been living together for ten years. She'll be so excited! We recently got in a fight as she found porn on my computer and phone, but I'm so excited to share this good news with her." The pastor then said, "Are you going to join our church or look into becoming a new member?" The young man said, "No, I believe in Jesus Christ as my savior! I'm going to heaven! I won't be needing to join church. I am justified by faith! I was also baptized as an infant but left the church for about twenty years." There was an old man that had heard this whole conversation between the young man and the pastor and approached the young man and said with a smile, "Young man, it sounds like you need to be born again." The young man said, "What do you mean?" The old man put his arm around the young man's shoulder and said with a smile, "Young man, if you would let me take you out to eat, I'd be honored to share the gospel with you and explain what it means to be born again." And so, the young man took the old man up on his offer.

CHAPTER 16

Baptismal Regeneration: A Different Gospel

Galatians 1:8–9—But even if we, or an angel from heaven, should preach to you a gospel other than the one we have preached to you, he is to be accursed! As we have said before, even now I say again: If anyone is preaching to you a gospel contrary to what you received, he is to be accursed!

As was mentioned earlier in the book, if any man should preach another gospel, let that man be damned. Paul had no qualms about the danger of teaching a false gospel. Likewise, God the Holy Spirit inspired Paul to proclaim this condemnation on anyone who should preach another gospel. Additionally, Jesus was not quiet on this matter either. Jesus said in Matthew 18:6, "If anyone causes one of these little ones—those who believe in me—to stumble, it would be better for them to have a millstone hung around their neck and to be drowned in the depths of the sea." In other words, those who teach that you can look to your baptism as the grounds of salvation, eternal life, and receiving the Holy Spirit would be better off to have a large millstone hung around their neck and be drowned in the depths of the sea. In other words, you'd be much better off not teaching this doctrine and remaining silent than to continue to lead people astray by having them look to their baptism as a means of their salvation.

Jesus had more to say about teachers who would lead people astray. Jesus said in Matthew 23:13–15, "Woe to you, teachers of the law and Pharisees, you hypocrites! You shut the door of the kingdom of heaven in people's faces. You yourselves do not enter, nor will you let those enter who are trying to. Woe to you, teachers of the law and Pharisees, you hypocrites! You travel over land and sea to win a single convert, and when you have succeeded, you make them twice as much a child of hell as you are." In other words, as it relates to teaching baptismal regeneration, Jesus could just as well have said this, "Woe to you, The Lutheran Church—Missouri Synod, you hypocrites! You shut the door of the kingdom of heaven in people's faces by teaching baptismal regeneration which is a damning false gospel. You yourselves do not enter, nor will you let those enter who are trying to. Woe to you, The Lutheran Church—Missouri Synod, you have seminaries, churches, elementary schools, high schools, and mission teams that hold to this false gospel of baptismal regeneration and confuse and cause men to stumble. You travel over land and sea to win people to your denomination and when you do, you make them twice a child of hell!" Although The Lutheran Church—Missouri Synod will also teach justification by faith alone, they also teach that you are saved in your baptism. Baptismal regeneration and justification by faith alone are not compatible. In fact, they are enemies of each other. No true doctrine of justification by grace alone through faith alone in Christ alone can also have baptismal regeneration. A little yeast leavens the whole lump and baptismal regeneration is a condemnable false gospel which also leads to more doctrinal error. Let any church that teaches baptismal regeneration heed this warning.

There is no doubt that Martin Luther played a tremendous role in the birth of the Reformation. His contributions to the Christian faith were outstanding. He fought for grace alone through faith alone in Christ alone. He fought against indulgences. He fought against purgatory. He fought for Scripture alone. He stood his ground and stood for Christ when the Catholic church declared anathema on him. He translated the Bible from Latin to German. He was a man on fire for Christ. This book has nothing to do with smudging the importance of Luther or even declaring anathema on Luther for his doctrine of baptismal regeneration. However, this doctrine of baptismal regeneration is a false teaching and baptismal regeneration is a false gospel.

This book is not arguing against the baptism of infants as there is strong Biblical evidence to support the baptism of infants. This book is not declaring anathema or damnation on specific people, those who are in The Lutheran Church—Missouri Synod, or any other church that teaches baptismal regeneration or have taught it in years past as God is the final judge of all men. This book is not a means to disagree over the attributes of God, the Trinity, the person and work of Christ, or any other important doctrines. However, there is no doubt that baptismal regeneration is a false gospel. This book sought to explain the verses that have been used as a defense of baptismal regeneration and exposit the meaning of the Scriptural texts. When considering this book and the false gospel of baptismal regeneration or being saved through baptism, please consider the several points that have been made.

- Jesus' teaching of regeneration or being born from above (John 3:3)
- Jesus' teaching of being born of water and the Spirit (John 3:5, Ezekiel 36:24–27)
- Nicodemus would not have understood being born of water and the Spirit as Christian baptism as this had not yet been instituted and Jesus was not talking about performing

another ritual or sacramental ordinance to enter the kingdom of God. (John 3:5)

- Jesus' teaching on total depravity and flesh only producing flesh and sin (John 3:6)
- Jesus' teaching on the work of the Holy Spirit as being analogous to the wind, which is not controlled, coerced, or commanded (John 3:8)
- Jesus' teaching of the new birth, which is monergistic (John 3:1–10)
- The baptism of repentance for the forgiveness of sins as preached by John the Baptist was a radical call to repentance and not just another ritual. (Luke 3:3–16)
- The baptism of repentance didn't call for just being dipped in, sprinkled with, or immersed in water, but a heart-searching repentance that elevated sin, brought down pride and self-righteousness, called for acknowledgement that Jews were no better than Gentiles, and called for a complete turning away of one's life in preparation for the Messiah. (Luke 3:3–16)
- Matthew understood that John and all other men could only baptize with water, but Christ could baptize with the Holy Spirit. (Matthew 3:11–12)
- Mark understood that John and all other men could only baptize with water, but Christ could baptize with the Holy Spirit. (Mark 1:8)
- Luke understood that John and all other men could only baptize with water, but Christ could baptize with the Holy Spirit. (Luke 3:16)
- The apostle John understood that John and all other men could only baptize with water, but Christ could baptize with the Holy Spirit. (John 1:31–33)
- John the Baptist understood that he and all other men could only baptize with water, but Christ could baptize

with the Holy Spirit. (Matthew 3:11–12, Mark 1:8, Luke 3:16, John 1:31–33)

- Peter understood that he and all other men could only baptize with water, but Christ could baptize with the Holy Spirit. (Acts 2:17–18, 10:44–48, 11:16)
- Jesus understood that only He could baptize with the Holy Spirit and that men could only baptize with water. (Matthew 3:11–12; Mark 1:8; Luke 3:16, 24:49; John 1:31–33, 7:38–39, 14:15–17, 14:26, 15:26, 16:7; Acts 1:4–5, 2:17–18, 10:44–48, 11:16)
- Jesus understood baptism as a work and not baptism as God working through the baptism. (Matthew 3:13–15)
- Paul's understanding of baptism with the Holy Spirit (1 Corinthians 12:13)
- Paul's understanding of the power and position of water baptism in contrast with preaching the gospel (1 Corinthians 1:14–30)
- Paul's understanding of sacraments or signs and seals of faith, which include baptism, and that they had no power to justify man (Romans 4:1–17)
- Paul's emphasis that if anyone relies on the law which includes works, rituals, sacraments, and ceremonies that they are alienated from Christ (Galatians 5:3-4)
- Christ's call to saving faith and entering through the narrow gate (Matthew 5:3–6, 10:37–39, 13:44–46; Mark 8:34–35; Luke 9:23–26, 14:25–33, 18:9–14; John 12:24–26)

Matthew, Mark, Luke, the apostle John, John the Baptist, the prophet Joel, Peter, Paul, and Jesus knew nothing of the Word being in with and under the water which made baptism effective for salvation. These men did not know of the Word, or any command being placed or connected with the water, which would make baptism effective for salvation. These men would not have agreed with the Holy Spirit being given in water baptism. These men made distinctions between water baptism and baptism with the Holy Spirit. These men knew that only Jesus baptized with the Holy Spirit.

Other Errors

One of the biggest issues that baptismal regeneration leads to is "easy believing." When the church teaches that its members are saved through baptism and the members show no signs of regeneration (John 3:1–10), the church becomes filled with false disciples (Matthew 7:21–23) and no distinction or warning is given. In fact, the unregenerate church member can be told that there is the hope in the fact that they were baptized. In fact, the doctrine of Biblical Regeneration has been replaced with the false gospel and doctrine of baptismal regeneration. Additionally, the call to repentance and saving faith is rarely or never given because there is no need for such a call when one has been baptized and is a member of the Lutheran Church. Much could be said about this, but this is one of the saddest outcomes of baptismal regeneration that I've seen. There are several other errors that baptismal regeneration leads to, but for the sake of this book, I will leave these unmentioned. The loving thing to do is to warn of this error as Paul says in 1 Corinthians 13:6, "Love does not delight in evil but rejoices with the truth." The loving thing is to warn of the false doctrine and false gospel as Paul said in Galatians 5:9, "A little yeast works through the whole batch of dough." Jesus warned His churches of holding to false teaching and urged the churches to repent or He would war against them (Revelation 2:14–15). Jesus warned against tolerating teaching that leads people astray and to repent of this work (Revelation 2:20–21). Jude tells us to be merciful to those who teach false doctrine but to do so with fear (Jude 23). This false gospel of baptismal regeneration needs to be repented of. It is at war with justification by grace alone, through faith alone, in Christ alone. Baptismal regeneration is at war with the gospel of Jesus Christ.

Conclusion

My prayer is that this book is not used to destroy The Lutheran Church—Missouri Synod or any other church that holds to this teaching. However, this book should be used as exhortation, rebuke, and encouragement to reform this doctrine of baptismal regeneration as there are eternal dangers to one who clings to the hope of their baptism rather than on Christ alone. Additionally, there is a strong warning that comes from God that if any man should preach another gospel, let God damn that man. Paul argues vehemently against clinging to anything else than Christ through faith in Galatians.

Prayerfully consider this book. Share it with loved ones. Pray for the church leaders of the LCMS as well as other churches who teach this. Preach Christ crucified. Preach the Narrow Gate. Preach Christ's call to discipleship and saving faith. Preach repentance. Preach the gospel of salvation by grace alone through faith alone in Christ alone. Preach the new birth or regeneration. Christ loves His church and will work out all things according to the counsel of His will. May this book be used for the edification of the saints.

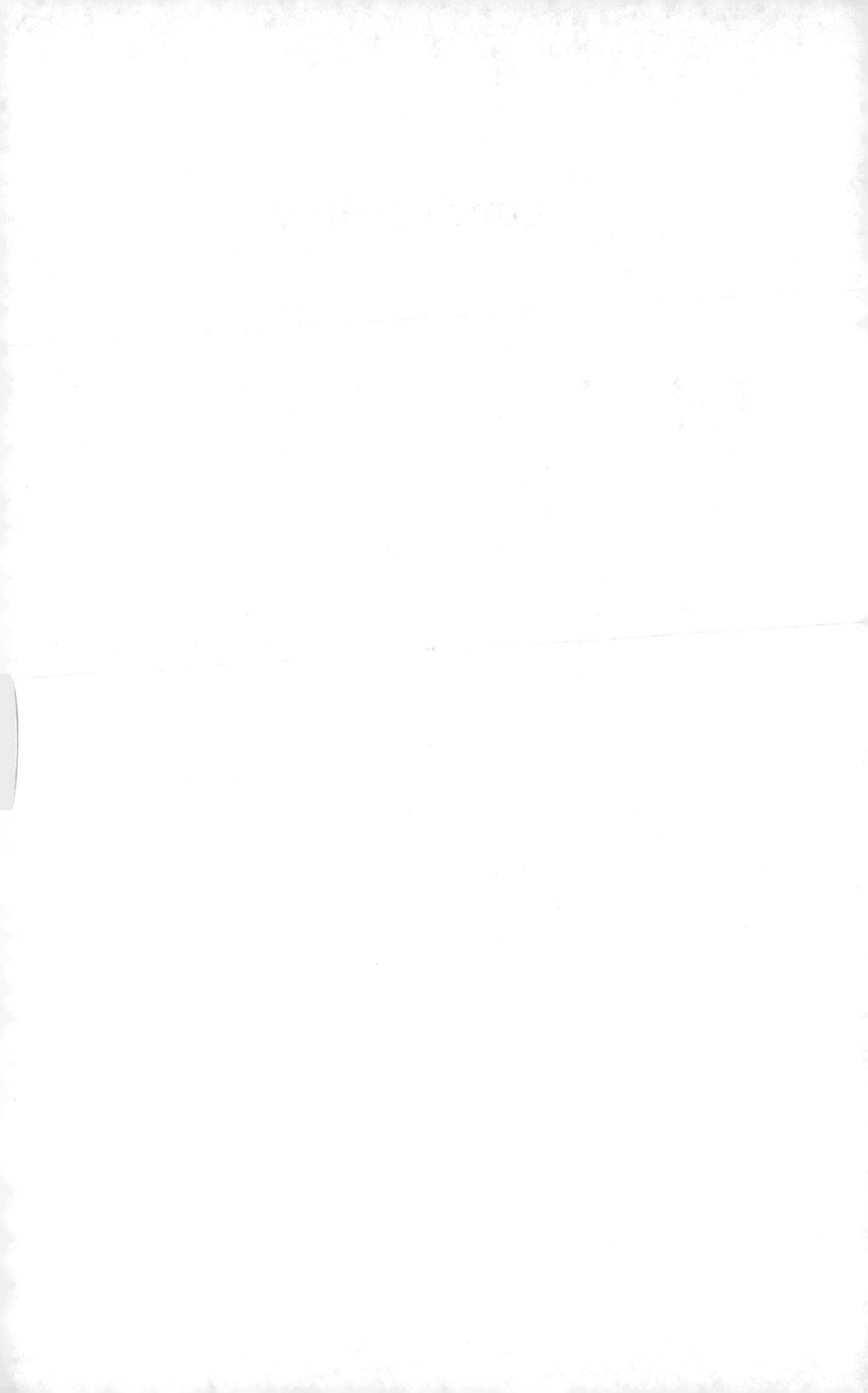

Bibliography

Kolb, Robert and Timothy J. Wengert. *The Book of Concord: The Confessions of the Evangelical Lutheran Church.* Translated by Charles P. Arand. Pennsylvania: Fortress Press, 2000.

Luther, Martin. "Martin Luther's Definition of Faith: An excerpt from 'An Introduction to St. Paul's Letter to the Romans,'" *Luther's German Bible of 1522.*

___. *Luther's Small Catechism with Explanation.* Missouri: Concordia Publishing House, 1986.